THE QUALITY/PROFIT CONNECTION

THE QUALITY/PROFIT CONNECTION

CONNECTION

H. James Harrington

American Society for Quality Control
310 West Wisconsin Avenue
Milwaukee, Wisconsin 53203

THE QUALITY/PROFIT CONNECTION

H. James Harrington

Published by American Society for Quality Control • Milwaukee

Copyright © 1989 by American Society for Quality Control

ISBN 0-87389-033-7

Printed in the United States of America

This book is dedicated to three good friends who have helped guide and support me as I developed and grew in the quality field. They are Mr. Walter L. Hurd, Jr., Dr. Armand V. Feigenbaum, and Dr. Walter Masing.

TABLE OF CONTENTS

INTRODUCTION

THE QUEST FOR QUALITY

World War III has begun. This time, it is not a war of battleships, bullets, and bombs. This is an economic war, and the weapons are TVs, steel, cars, and clothes. This is a war where we have no allies, as every country in the world is out to capture more than its share of the United States and world markets. We are being attacked with tires from Brazil, cars from Japan, radios from Taiwan, clothes from Britain, cosmetics from France, shoes from Italy, and beef from Argentina and Australia.

American business entered the 1980s with a deep-seated resolution to stop the flood of imported products, and as a result, a group of new admirals and generals took over to reestablish our industrial leadership. These are people like John Akers of IBM, F. James McDonald of General Motors, Jim Olson of AT&T, and John Young of Hewlett-Packard. Industrial leaders like these are laying out the strategies and providing the thrust to lead the United States back to the prominence it once had. But it will take a long time to reestablish and reposition American industry. It cannot be accomplished overnight. It takes years to reestablish a reputation once it has been destroyed or, at the very least, tarnished.

Causes of the War

During the three decades following World War II, American business virtually had a monopoly in the world market. Our international competition was bombed out or had become obsolete, making it impossible for them to compete in price or quality. Customers around the world were starved for products that they had been deprived of during the war. It was a seller's market and almost anything that was produced could be sold.

Everything was going our way. There was a high demand for our products around the world. Our standard of living was improving yearly. We were feeding a hungry world with our farm and industrial products. We were the world's showplace. Large groups of business people toured our country to marvel at our management systems and our production facilities. We sent our young and our experienced people around the world to help other countries learn our ways and techniques so they could be more productive and could buy more of our toasters, radios, computers, and airplanes.

We thought we had nothing to fear from foreign competition. Sure, the Volkswagen Beetle had made some inroads, but Asia was viewed as a producer of cheap copies of U.S. products that would never be able to compete

1

in our marketplace, and boastfully we told the world so. John Foster Dulles, U.S. Secretary of State, in discussions on September 12, 1954, told Japanese Prime Minister Yoshida, "Frankly, Japan should not expect to find a big U.S. market because the Japanese don't make the things we want." *Business Week* predicted in 1968 that the Japanese auto industry would not "carve out a big slice" of the U.S. market. The world market was our mistress, and our romance was hot and heavy. The year 1978 was America's industrial Pearl Harbor. Suddenly this huge, sleeping, overconfident, boastful nation realized that the developing economic trends were leading the nation into economic disaster. As Douglas D. Danforth, chairman of Westinghouse Corporation, put it, "In 1979 there was ample evidence that quality had become a powerful weapon in the hands of a number of foreign competitors."

Foreign Competition

The Japanese, after World War II, were faced with a complex problem. Not only were their factories destroyed, but their strong conglomerate structures were forcefully disbanded by the occupational forces. They were literally starting over from scratch. With this new start, they realized that they would have to carve out a new niche for themselves in the international business community; they could not prosper and improve their standard of living if they were to continue to produce cheap imitations of Western products. They saw that they needed to change their international reputation by demonstrating that they could produce high-quality products priced competitively with Western-made products. With this in mind, they viewed America's management system from a different angle. They realized that American business schools completely missed the subject of quality. They carefully avoided the lessons that were being taught in the MBA programs, directing their attention to the process of manufacturing and understanding how to control it. Yes, America had a lot to offer, but it was not what was being taught in the MBA schools.

Slowly, ever so slowly at first, Japanese products began to change. Like a thundercloud off in the distance, the warnings were there. But American managers never turned to look over their shoulders. The sun was shining and business was prospering. Around the mid-1960s we began to feel the first raindrops. By the beginning of the 1970s other countries began to follow Japan's lead, and by the middle of the 1970s we were flooded with products from around the world. Many American products not only failed to compete in the international market, but could not even compete at home — most notably, the family car. The *U.S.S. Arizona* of World War III can be compared to the auto industry, where 25.7 percent of the new cars sold in the United States during 1985 were imported, and this will increase to over 40 percent by 1990. The average U.S. auto has 2.5 defects during the first year of warranty compared to 1.3 for the average Japanese car and 1.9 for a Mercedes-Benz. The first year's warranty cost for Japanese cars is $55, while U.S. manufacturers pay between $100 and $400.

Automobiles are not the only battle we are losing — foreign manufacturers are attacking products as unlikely as cement, where in the period from 1980 to 1986 foreign producers almost tripled their share of the U.S. market, going from 6.5 percent in 1980 to an estimated 18 percent in 1986. By 1985 imports had captured 77 percent of the U.S. nonrubber footwear market, up from 41 percent in 1975 (data from U.S. Department of Commerce). Foreign sales of textiles and clothing increased from $4.0 billion in 1975 to $19.4 billion in 1984 (*U.S. News & World Report*, Nov. 18, 1985, p. 47). That's a lot of meat and potatoes taken off the plates of American households.

In response to this invasion from overseas, American corporations spent the late 1970s and early 1980s reexamining corporate values. American business-men discovered:

- They had lost touch with their customers.
- Short-term profits had replaced long-term market shares.
- Both quality and productivity growth rates were falling, not keeping pace with those of many other countries.
- Employee loyalty was a thing of the past.
- The American dollar was overvalued throughout the world.
- Inflation and high interest rates were stifling the economy.
- Product cost could no longer be increased to hide the staggering cost of poor quality and inadequate manufacturing and business systems.

As a result:

- Foreign-made products were taking larger and larger shares of internal and external markets.
- Unemployment rates were out of control.
- Absenteeism and turnover rates were cutting deeply into profits.
- The balance of trade had become unfavorable.
- R&D spending had been reduced to make the quarterly reports look bet-ter, making the future look black — or red, if you are looking at the company's future financial outlook.
- American product reputation had sunk to an all-time low.

It was apparent that three actions were required to salvage our lagging economy and correct our distorted balance of trade. We needed to (1) meet customer expectations, (2) improve productivity and quality, and (3) restruc-ture management methods and priorities. American management in the 1960s and 1970s thought it knew what the customer needed better than the customer did and set about to give it to them, while our foreign competitors set about to satisfy their expectations.

As we entered the 1980s, it was obvious to most managers that something was wrong with the present U.S. management system and the curriculum being taught in business schools around the country. The values that had made

America great had shifted. Short-range profits were driving our management systems and taking priority over customers' needs. Company loyalty was a thing of the past. We were well on our way to becoming a second-rate industrial power. Tom Peters, analyzing the reason high-tech companies in the United States are having problems, said, "It is management's inability or unwillingness to shift from a technology-centered to a customer-centered organization."

The market had changed from a sellers' to a consumers' market, and the customer not only wanted quality, but demanded it. Business leaders suddenly realized what our forefathers had always known — the customer is king, and survival is based on satisfying the customer's expectations.

Customers have three perspectives about everything they buy: needs, expectations, and desires. For example, a traveler's needs are fulfilled by a Motel 6, for it provides a clean room, a bed, and a bath. Their expectations are met by a room at the Hyatt Regency, and their desires are fulfilled with a suite at the top of Caesar's Palace in Las Vegas.

If you satisfy only your customers' needs you will not have dissatisfied customers, but you will have no assurance that they will ever return. To have a loyal customer, you need to meet expectations and do more than just the basics — you need to make it a pleasure to do business with you. That is the only way to keep a customer. Too many companies look at an individual sale as the end of an activity. It is really an opportunity to start a life-long relationship. That is the way to build a business, to capture a larger portion of the market, and to ensure long-term success of your company. Customers who value your products are your company's best asset, for they ensure your future. First, they are far easier to sell additional products to, and second, they provide your best advertising campaign. You do not need to satisfy your customers' desires, because all of us need a goal to strive for, something that is out of the ordinary, a goal that may never be reached, or at best, seldom attained. But never, never stop with meeting your customers' needs. Go further to know, understand, and provide products and services that fulfill their expectations.

Donald E. Peterson, chairman of the board of Ford Motor Company, said, "World-class quality means providing products and services that meet customer needs and expectations at a cost that represents value to the customer." Value — that's a beautiful word. It combines quality and price in the customer's mind. When customers' requirements are met they will not complain, but they may not come back to buy your product again if another product is equally available. When you provide your customers with a product or service that they value, however, you have a customer for life. Or, in the words of John A. Young, president of Hewlett-Packard, "Satisfying customers is the only reason we are in business."

Protectionism

Every country around the world has its eyes on the American market. The Commerce Department estimates that 70 percent of all American manufactured products are potential targets for foreign competition. Even our own companies are building in yen and selling in dollars. Imports are costing much more than most Americans think. Each imported car, television, computer, or shirt has a ripple effect on the economy. The March 3, 1986 issue of *Business Week* reported that for each $1 billion of foreign-made automobiles, the cost to the U.S. economy was $2.43 billion. That makes a $10,000 Toyota cost $24,300 — not such a good buy after all.

The unprecedented trade deficit and its impact on the economy has brought about calls for more protectionism from management and organized labor. But protectionism is not the answer, because the cure is worse than the disease. According to the Institute for International Economics, protectionism cost American consumers over $56 billion in 1984. When you look at consumer cost to save a job because we were not competitive in the world market, the results, shown as follows, are staggering:

Industry	Cost/Job Saved
Automobiles	$ 105,000
Benzenoid chemicals	1,000,000
Carbon steel	750,000
Specialty steel	1,000,000
Dairy products	220,000
Orange juice	240,000
Textiles and apparel	42,000

Since 1980, the U.S. government has taken action to restrict imports on such items as motorcycles, steel, textiles, apparel, and building materials. The European Economic Community limits imports on such items as steel, automobiles, and electronic equipment. Canada has put restraints on textiles, apparel, automobiles, and footwear. Japan restricts imports of such items as footwear, leather, pharmaceuticals, textiles, apparel, and automobiles.

Typical U.S. trade barriers are:

- Peanuts — imports limited to less than one tenth of one percent consumption.
- Sugar — 2.5 million short tons per year.
- Heavy motorcycles — current tariff 20 percent of sales price.
- Clothes — 26 percent tariff plus restrictions on volume.
- Meats — import levels vary with U.S. cattle slaughter rate.
- Carbon steel — limited to one fifth of the U.S. market.

We must remember what the 1930 Smoot-Hawley tariff did to the world. It triggered retaliatory action in Europe that provoked the collapse of world trade, turning a slump into a worldwide depression. Although most Americans believe that Japan is being used as a scapegoat for our own economic problems (only 30 percent see Japan as competing unfairly), 63 percent favor some type of sanctions on Japanese goods (*New York Times*, August 13, 1985, p. 1). This alarming wave of protectionism is particularly important because it is not directed at one or two countries, but has become a worldwide strategy directed at protecting internal industries, taking away their incentive to compete in a fair, open market. We cannot afford the present balance of trade and we cannot afford protectionism. What we can afford and must provide is a fair, open market and American products that set the world standard for quality and value.

Keys to Improvement

The improvement process must become part of your management system. As Harold A. Poling, president of Ford Motor Company put it, "Continuous improvement in everything that is done is what it will take to continue to satisfy the customer."

What are the keys to the improvement process?

- Top management must believe the company can improve and must personally participate in the improvement process by setting the example.
- Remember that the customer is king. The company exists only to serve the customer. No customer, no business. No business, no jobs.
- Develop a preventative operating environment directed at eliminating or, at the very least, greatly reducing the need to react to "fires."
- Develop a company-wide desire to be the best, to be better today than you were yesterday, and better tomorrow than you are today.
- Develop a total management and employee understanding, active personal participation,and a belief that the results of the improvement process will benefit the employees, management, company, and customers.
- Establish a single standard of error-free performance.
- Remember that all departments and individuals have customers either inside or outside the business, who must have their expectations satisfied.
- Never compromise quality for cost or schedule.
- Understand that employees are not the problem, but can be part of the solution.
- Make effective use of employee skills, both physical and mental.
- Remember that a people-building philosophy will provide spectacular results, but a people-using philosophy will bring failure to the company.
- Remember that training is not expensive. In the long run, it is ignorance that is expensive.

- Understand that 85 percent of the problems can be corrected only by management.
- Understand that the improvement principles apply to every part of the business, not just to manufacturing.
- Ensure that both the individual and the team are given the opportunity to contribute to the success of the company and that the employees are rewarded for their contributions.
- Ensure that your company has a comprehensive, long-range improvement strategy *and* a short-range plan.

The Improvement Team

Productivity improvement and its twin, quality improvement, are now national, bipartisan issues. Although up to now there has been more talk than action, the fact that we are achieving a consensus is important because productivity and quality improvement will require teamwork among groups that have often competed with one another in the past. For example, we would have expected business leaders and economists to be concerned with the effect on productivity of tax reforms like those proposed by President Ronald Reagan, by Senator Bill Bradley and Representative Thomas Gephart, and by Senator Bob Kasten and Representative Jack Kemp. We might not have expected the same concern from a liberal columnist like David Broder. Yet Broder listed productivity, along with progressivism, principle, and effect on poverty, as primary criteria by which any tax reform should be evaluated.

The automobile industry provides another good example of teamwork. Ten years ago who could have imagined General Motors launching a subsidiary and telling it specifically to develop a corporate culture based on cooperation — let alone inviting the United Auto Workers Union to help plan the project in the earliest stages? That is a dramatic example, but it is not the only one. It is sad to observe the level of confrontation that still dominates the relationship between labor and management in some industries — even some parts of the auto industry — but General Motor's Saturn is a sign of what is possible if we work together.

As important as teamwork is on a national level, it is also somewhat abstract. It's one thing for United Auto Workers Vice President Donald Ephlin to stand up at a press conference with General Motors Chairman of the Board Roger Smith and General Motors President F. James McDonald; it's another thing for a supervisor and a shop steward to keep a common vision despite the day-to-day problems that arise in any job. The teamwork we are talking about here is of a different sort: not grand gestures, but constant attention to detail; not huge triumphs, but small steps; not press conferences, but talks at the water cooler; not trips to Washington, but a steady presence on the factory floor; not a private handshake, but a public willingness to try new ways to cooperate and understand.

Here is where productivity and quality meet. Quality improvement is an issue of national concern, but it is one that must be addressed to a large extent as an issue internal to each company. Quality is execution, attention to detail, steadiness of purpose. None of this happens in a vacuum — quality must become part of the fabric of the corporate as well as the national way of life. But though corporate personality may depend largely on senior management, it is not the product of edicts or proclamations. Rather it comes from action. If you want your employees to take quality seriously, you cannot ship out marginal products just to meet schedules.

Remember to involve employees in the improvement plans, for Americans support what they help to create. If they are not involved in the creation, they will wait to see if it can be successfully implemented without their help. Labor is doing its share to help put the United States back on top. Between 1979 and 1984, work stoppages involving 1,000 or more workers dropped from 235 to 56, even though the average annual negotiated pay raise dropped from 6.0 percent to 2.8 percent (U.S. Department of Labor data).

Management: The Problem and the Solution

In a 1986 Gallup survey conducted for the American Society for Quality Control, top U.S. executives rated employee attitudes (75 percent) as the chief detractor or inhibitor to quality. Other detractors, in descending order, were employee training, outside economic factors, outdated technology, and unions. These results typify managers who are looking for a scapegoat, who do not realize that employees exist in a system that management created and they (the employees) are hamstrung by its many inadequacies. Management has created employees' attitudes through years of neglect, dishonesty, and abuse. The employee is not the problem; management is.

The improvement process starts with upper management, is led by upper management, and is the responsibility of upper management. They have to believe there is a better way of doing things, that errors are not a normal way of doing business, and that errors can be prevented. Upper management has to write the script that will lead the company from a reaction to a prevention system.

Few of the problems that face companies today can or should be solved by top management, because the information and expertise needed to solve these problems reside much lower in the organization and because the problems are evolving continually. Top management's job is not to spot and solve problems, but to develop an organization that can spot and solve problems before they are out of control.

Once middle and first-line managers have the script in hand, they will understand that their role is not to direct, but to lead and coach employees, emphasizing the employees' strengths and helping to overcome their weaknesses, and encouraging them to give their best performance. The job of these managers is to extend the quality system from the board room to the boiler room. This can be accomplished only when management provides the following:

- The proper props — tools, equipment, and materials.
- The script — job description, operating procedures, and designs.
- Rehearsal time — training.
- Inspiration and perspiration — setting the example and providing the recognition.
- The stage — the work environment and the time to do the job right every time.
- Support — manufacturing, engineering, finance, drafting, and marketing.
- Audience understanding — communicating customer expectations.
- Encouragement — setting performance standards and encouraging employees to improve continuously.
- The audience — the customers.

Then, and only then, can the lights dim and the curtain go up. When the final curtain falls on the first performance, management must share the spotlight and the rewards with the employees to ensure a continuing high level of performance. Without all these elements, there is no chance for a play — or a business — to succeed.

Breaking Bureaucracy's Back

Management must lead an attack against the bureaucracy that has crept into the systems controlling the business. Bureaucracy in government and business is getting worse. It is building huge paperwork empires that must be destroyed if the United States is to survive. Our copiers are used far too much, and we have too many file cabinets. In 1955, the entire specification for the F-4 airplane produced by McDonnell Douglas Corporation was documented on two pages. In 1980, the proposal for the C-17 airplane consisted of 92 books containing 13,516 pages and 35,077 pieces of art. We need documentation, but just adding volume does not make it good. For example:

Document	Number of Words
Lord's Prayer	57
Ten Commandments	71
Gettysburg Address	266
Declaration of Independence	300
U.S. Government Contractor Management System Evaluation Program	38,000

(B.A. Hardesty, at 1985 Streamlining/Tailoring Conference)

In Boeing's manufacturing division, a team attacked the paperwork bureaucracy and cut six manuals down to one that was smaller than any of the previous six.

Changes Made from Lessons Learned

Let's take a close look at some of the key changes that have taken place since American industries awoke and found that they had a major quality and productivity problem.

- Members of top management have become much more aware of their role in directing the quality movement within their company. They have taken the quality-leadership role away from quality assurance and accepted it as their own responsibility.
- To ensure a quick, effective reaction to the challenge of competition, many companies have established an improvement steering council that is responsible for developing and implementing the improvement process within the company.
- Because management is the only group that can correct 85 percent of the company's problems, first emphasis has been placed on providing management with awareness of the importance of quality to the company and then providing management with a tool that would allow them to improve quality and productivity.
- The Japanese quality circle movement proved beyond a doubt the importance of team activities. As a result, quality circles, improvement teams, and quality of work life programs have spread like the measles through these companies. Management personalities have changed and participative management methods have been taught and practiced extensively.
- Teams are not the total answer because employees in the United States are individuals and like to achieve and be recognized as individuals. They have also realized that the employee works 39 hours a week as an individual solving problems and providing output but only one hour per week as a team member. Sure, they exist as part of a department team, but they work as individuals. This means that the company has to concentrate on involving each individual in the company's improvement process, ensuring that there is a direct relationship between their contribution and the recognition and reward system. Employees have been provided with the four T's:

  Training so they can do their job right every time.
  Tools so the process is capable of producing a quality product or service.
  Time so they can be sure the job is done right every time.
  Teams to support them in their efforts to do the job right.

- Companies have found that they need to concentrate on the systems that create or allow errors to occur. Error-free products and services can be accomplished only by focusing on the business process that controls the activities in both the white- and blue-collar areas.

- A new, closer working relationship has been developed between purchaser and supplier. They have both realized that they are interdependent. Purchasing agents have begun to recognize that low-ball pricing cannot offset poor quality. This new relationship is making business associates out of the old suppliers. Big businesses are providing their smaller brethren with education, long-term contracts, incentive programs, single-source contracts, and involving them in component-application decisions.

- Emphasis has been placed on aligning accountability with responsibility. Each area is starting to accept the accountability and responsibility for its output. This focus on quality as part of everyone's responsibility has expanded the quality program into every corner of the business. From the board room to the boiler room, from employment to development, from accounting to sales, new quality systems and measurement programs are being implemented. More attention is being focused on preventing problems, and as a result, reaction efforts are not required as often. This has stopped the disproportionate growth of quality control, inspection, and quality engineers. Today, more and more companies are using their quality workforce as a proactive rather than a reactive organization.

- Companies are reorganizing their top management structures to put quality at the same organizational level as engineering, production, and finance. This has been done to show all employees that quality is the most critical issue in today's environment.

- Quality is not like tomorrow. You cannot just wait for it and expect it to come to you. It requires a well-thought-out, detailed, documented plan that is totally agreed upon by all areas in the company.

- For too long the U.S. recognition system has been directed toward individuals who react to fires and not to the people who prevent them. There has also been an important need to provide a recognition system that includes personal, public, and financial recognition for employees who contribute to the success of the company. These requirements have made it necessary to restructure many recognition systems to focus benefits on the prevention and improvement processes.

Can America Win in the Marketplace? Yes!

In spite of the many negative indicators, the pendulum has begun to swing in America's direction. In 1985, U.S. corporations accounted for 11 of the world's largest industrial corporations, ranked by sales. General Motors heads this list, followed by Exxon in second place. A number of other American companies are leading the way. These winning companies search out opportunities, understand the culture and politics of other countries, study the needs, wants, and desires of the potential customers, and adapt their products to fill those needs, carving out their own corner of the international market.

In doing this, many American companies are outselling the Japanese in Japan as well as the rest of the world. An average of four U.S. companies a week receive licenses in Japan. By the end of 1985, more than 2,300 U.S. companies had $3.2 billion invested in their business in Japan, making Japan our number one overseas investment location by a factor of seven times its nearest competitor. Typical companies that generate a major portion of their revenue outside of the United States are Boeing, Kellogg, IBM, Coca-Cola, and McDonald's. Hewlett-Packard earned $304 million in profits from $2.8 billion in sales outside of the United States in 1985. IBM's estimated profits from Japan alone ran about $600 million in 1985. For the past 10 years, Avon sales have grown at an annual rate of more than 25 percent. Kellogg realizes about 30 percent of their gross sales overseas every year. Coca-Cola has 60 percent of the Japanese soft drink market and Schick supplies Japan with about 70 percent of its razors. McDonald's has more than 2,000 restaurants outside of the United States (500 outlets in Japan alone), and the restaurants in Japan and Latin America are among the biggest money-makers in their system.

The key to success in the Japanese market is to know your customer. (And isn't that true in any market?) To meet consumer needs in Japan, Johnson and Johnson makes its toothbrushes shorter and rounder at the top and its baby lotion less greasy. Johnson and Johnson's sales in Japan were about $67 million in 1985.

Both Kentucky Fried Chicken and McDonald's restaurants nearly failed in Japan before they realized they needed to locate their establishments where pedestrian traffic abounds rather than in suburban drive-in locations. In addition, McDonald's altered standards for its hamburgers, adding more onions and fat to suit Japanese taste buds while the Colonel added more soy sauce to his secret recipe. The results? Sales in Japan for 1985 were $705 million for McDonald's and $350 million for Kentucky Fried Chicken. Fox Bagel, Ltd. found that American bagels were too large for the Japanese appetite. As a result, the bagels they sell in Japan are smaller and softer.

Dunkin Donuts found that the American store layout would not bring in Japanese customers. Success came to the company when they provided a coffee-house environment. Why? Because they were not just selling a product, but also a service. In 1985 their Japanese sales were $250 million.

Victor Harris, president of Max Factor's Japanese activities, said, "A compact that does not open and close smoothly is guaranteed to flop in the Japanese market, where the standards of packaging are higher than anywhere in the world."

Japanese customers who tend to buy American-made goods are college educated, wealthier, and between 18 and 29 years old. This is the reason such products as Tiffany jewelry, Bausch and Lomb Ray-ban sunglasses, MacGregor golf equipment, Nike shoes, and Ralph Lauren polo shirts attract the Japanese buyer.

At a time when many American companies are turning to Japanese companies to buy less expensive, high-quality products to sell under their brand name, IBM is selling copiers to Konica Business Machines who then slap their label on. Japanese automobiles manufactured in the United States are being shipped to countries like Taiwan and back to Japan.

The number-one rule for success in the Japanese market then, and for that matter in any market, is to know your customers' needs, expectations, and desires personally, and be sure that your products fully live up to them. As these companies demonstrate day in and day out, American companies have not lost all of their competitive instinct.

Examples of Change

IBM started to buy memory chips for the 3081 CPU outside the company because the quality was equivalent and the price was lower than they could produce in-house. This set the IBM Burlington, Vermont, plant into action, and today all the memory chips used in the new IBM 3090 are manufactured internally. In the early days IBM's personal computer was made up of many purchased components. Today, these high-technology units are manufactured internally: keyboards from Lexington, Kentucky, disk drives from Rochester, Minnesota, printers from Charlotte, North Carolina. Why? Because IBM knew that it could produce higher quality products at less cost internally using American labor and know-how.

At IBM in Endicott, New York, improvement efforts, which included a massive modernization of their manufacturing facility, resulted in decreasing the number of manufacturing steps required to build large circuit boards by 50 percent. Output has doubled and costs have decreased 20 percent per year, while the product quality has shown a marked improvement. For the past two years, there has not been a single board with an open or shorted circuit. Of IBM's three-year (1986-89) capital budget, approximately one third is earmarked for improving manufacturing facilities. Jack Kuehler, senior vice-president of IBM, when talking about the need to invest in developing new manufacturing methods, said, "It's not clear to me that companies can't keep their lead in manufacturing also." He warns, "Once you are behind, it's very hard to catch up" *(Business Week,* June 16, 1986, p. 106).

Chrysler Corporation shows what can be done when the team works together. In 1979 Chrysler required a $1.2 billion federal loan grant to stay in production. Today, Chrysler's gross profit per vehicle is the highest of the Big 3, varying between $1,500 and $1,650. The table shows the results of their effort *(USA Today,* June 2, 1986, p. 2B).

	1979	**1985**
Annual income	−$1.1 billion	+$1.6 billion
Stock price — high	7-3/4	31-3/8
Stock price — low	3-3/4	19-7/8
Sales	$11.4 billion	$21.3 billion

These success stories are useful in several ways. Like old *Lives of the Saints*, they provide us with models of good corporate behavior. And if in this sense quality is a virtue, they show us the reward for virtuous behavior.

Traits of Successful Companies

Improving quality and productivity, meeting customer expectations, being better today than you were yesterday — that is what this book is all about. The chapters record a series of interviews with top management in some of the companies that have led the way in making a significant improvement in the quality of their products. These chapters review the details of these improvement processes and provide case studies of actual improvements in quality and productivity, thereby reducing costs. As you look at these case studies, remember that improvement consists of a myriad of small steps as we move closer and closer to our ultimate goal of error-free performance. It cannot be accomplished in one giant step where a company goes from poor to outstanding or even from good to outstanding by making a single or even a small number of changes.

As I studied these companies and a number of other companies that have successfully implemented improvement processes around the world, some very important trends developed. These are what I call the "16 Golden Traits" of companies that have successful improvement processes. Such successful companies pay attention to the following:

1. *Close customer relationships.* They maintain close personal contact with their customers to ensure understanding of the customers' changing needs and expectations. When problems arise, they react quickly, pouring oil on the troubled waters.
2. *Concern for the individual employee.* They respect the individual's rights and dignity, realizing that the company succeeds only to the degree that the individual succeeds. They respect the individual's thoughts and ideas, realizing that he or she has more to contribute to the company than just physical labor. They not only encourage the participation of the employee, they require it. They look at the individual as part of the solution to their problems, not as the problem.
3. *Top management leadership of the quality process.* Members of top management in the company have accepted their role in leading the

quality activities of the company. Support groups such as quality assurance provide advice, research problems, and provide data. But the company president sets the direction and establishes the standards. These company presidents realize that their company is an image of themselves, and they understand that they must set the personal quality example.

4. *High standards.* These companies set extremely high standards for their products, services, and people. They strive to set the standard for their industry and are dissatisfied if they are not number one.

5. *Understanding the importance of the team.* They use teams to unite the company, improve working relationships, and improve morale. They understand that only management can solve 85 percent of the problems and that employee teams are required to attack the other 15 percent.

6. *Effort to meet and exceed customer expectations.* They are not satisfied with the state of the art and are always trying to provide better products and services to their customers and at lower cost. They understand their customers' needs and go beyond them to fulfill their expectations, realizing that just fulfilling the customers' needs will not capture future sales. They want their output to be valued by their customers.

7. *Belief that quality is first priority.* When a compromise between quality, cost, or schedule must be made, quality is never compromised. They realize that poor quality causes most of their cost and schedule problems and that if they focus their attention on the quality problems, their cost and schedule problems will take care of themselves. They also realize that the quality personality of the company is extremely fragile, particularly during the change period, and that even the smallest compromise in quality can set back progress many years.

8. *View of business for the long term.* Top management realizes that the important objectives are directed at the long-term survival and prosperity of the company. They give priority to the long-range plans that will build a product and customer base, paying secondary attention to quarterly and yearly reports. They measure their success by their company's long-term growth, not by short-term fluctuations over which they often have little or no control.

9. *Sharing of prosperity with the employees.* They look at the employees as partners and establish programs that directly relate the success of the company to the employees' earnings and their contributions. Programs like gain sharing, suggestion, and pay for performance are key parts of the employee benefit package.

10. *Management and employee education.* They realize that education is not expensive; it is ignorance that is costly. These companies have realized that everyone is responsible for quality and that everyone needs education related to the quality tools if they are to meet this responsibility. As a result, heavy focus on quality education has been directed at the

management team and key professionals. At the employee level, education has been directed at problem-solving methods and job training.

11. *Management leadership rather than supervision.* They realize that management must be leaders of the employees rather than dictators. It is much easier to pull a string in the desired direction than to push it. For management to assume the leadership role has not been easy, and many of the companies are still working on this change in their company personality. After all, for the past 40 years we have trained our managers to be attack dogs, and now we want them to be purring kittens.

12. *Investment in the future.* Research and development means investing in the future of the company. It ensures a steady flow of products and ideas needed to meet the expectations of the future market. Along with the need for research, a parallel need is to provide the employees with equipment that pushes the state of the art and allows them to perform at their very best. Companies that realize this have prospered. Those that have not, failed or will eventually fail.

13. *Focus on the business system.* They realize that the only way to prevent errors from occurring is by correcting the business system that controls the company activities. Employees work *in* the business system, while managers must work *on* the system.

14. *Recognition systems.* These companies realize that recognition takes many forms — financial, personal, and public. They have established a recognition system with many options to ensure that it meets the total needs of employees and management. A pat on the back is good, but sometimes a pat on the wallet is better and more appropriate. On other occasions, a personal letter sent to the employee's home is the best action.

15. *Employee involvement.* These companies go out of their way to make all the employees feel that they are part of the business and that their contributions are important. They take time to involve the employees in their long-range plans and report progress back to them periodically. They make them part of the company by providing such things as a stock-purchase plan or gain sharing. They provide the employees with opportunities to meet and understand customers, the ones who receive their output. Sometimes a customer is outside the company, but more often it is another company employee. It is not easy to care about customers when you never see or hear from them, but if the customer is the person who sits behind you or in the next office, the whole concept of customer satisfaction becomes a much more personal issue.

16. *Decreased bureaucracy.* Management continuously works at making all decisions at the lowest level. Maximum authority is given to each level of management. Checks and balances are used, but only when absolutely necessary. Management realizes that bureaucracy has a tendency to work its way into the business systems, and they are continuously vigilant to minimize its impact.

Summary

Extensive research has proven that improved perceived product quality is the most effective way to increase profits and the most important factor in the long-term profitability of a company. American business is beginning to believe in the value of quality and to back its belief with action. It is a first step down that long road to regain our market share, to reestablish the United States as the standard-setter for the world. It is a race to satisfy expectations of customers around the world. The improvement process will provide your company with the competitive edge to put it ahead of the pack. Don't be left at the starting gate. Remember, you can't win today's race with last week's press clippings.

The race is not over yet. The United States is making progress, but we still have a long way to go to recapture the reputation we had in the 1960s. The only way we can do it is by working together and never being satisfied with how good we are.

H. James Harrington, PhD
President
Harrington, Hurd & Squires Group
Los Gatos, California

Ford Motor Company

Corporate Background

Ford Motor Company entered the business world without fanfare on June 16, 1903, when the late Henry Ford and 11 associates filed incorporation papers in Lansing, Michigan. With an abundance of faith and only $28,000 in cash, the pioneering industrialists gave birth to what was to become one of the world's largest corporations.

At the time of its incorporation, Ford was a tiny operation in a converted Detroit wagon factory staffed with 10 people. Today, the company is one of the world's largest industrial enterprises with active manufacturing, assembly, and sales operations in 29 countries on six continents. Ford is the second largest manufacturing company in the United States.

More than 380,000 men and women now come to work each day in Ford factories, laboratories, and offices around the world. Ford products are sold in nearly 150 nations and territories by a global network of some 13,200 dealers. The company's annual sales exceed the gross national products of many industrialized nations. For 19 consecutive years, Ford has sold more vehicles overseas than any other U.S.-based manufacturer.

Ford's first 19 years included the production of more than 15,000 Model Ts. By 1927, Ford Motor Company was a giant industrial complex that spanned the globe. Its cars had started an urban revolution. Its $5 day and the philosophy behind it had started a social revolution. Its moving assembly line had started an industrial revolution.

During those years of hectic expansion, Ford Motor Company:
- Began producing trucks and tractors (1917).
- Became wholly owned by Henry Ford and his son, Edsel, who succeeded his father as president after a conflict with stockholders over the millions to be spent to build the giant Rouge plant in Dearborn, Michigan (1919).
- Bought the Lincoln Motor Company (1922).

19

- Built the first of 196 Ford Tri-Motor airplanes used by America's first commercial airlines (1925).

Paralleling Ford's domestic growth has been an international expansion program which got its start in 1904, just one year after the company was formed. On August 17 of that year, a modest plant opened in Canada in the small town of Walkerville, Ontario, with the name of Ford Motor Company of Canada, Ltd. From this small beginning an overseas organization of manufacturing plants, assembly plants, parts depots, and dealers has grown around the world. About 40,000 companies in 45 countries supply Ford with goods and services.

Although Ford is better known as a manufacturer of cars and trucks, it now produces a wide range of other products including farm and industrial tractors, industrial engines, construction machinery, steel, glass, and plastics. Ford is established in a diversity of other businesses including finance, insurance, automotive replacement parts, electronics, communications, space technology, and land development.

Interview with James K. Bakken
Vice President, Operations Support Services

Do you have an official quality policy?

At Ford Motor Company, our Mission and Guiding Principles statement preceded our official quality policy. We're a customer-driven company and our mission is to improve our products and services continually to meet our customers' needs, allowing us to prosper as a business and to provide a reasonable return to our stockholders, the owners of our business. How we accomplish our mission is as important as the mission itself. Fundamental to success for the company are these basic values:

- *People.* Our people are the source of our strength. They provide our corporate intelligence and determine our reputation and vitality. Involvement and teamwork are core human values.
- *Products.* Our products are the end result of our efforts, and they should be the best in serving customers worldwide. As our products are viewed, so are we viewed.
- *Profits.* Profits are the ultimate measure of how efficiently we provide customers with the best products for their needs. Profits are required to survive and grow.

Our guiding principles are made up of these concepts:

- *Quality comes first.* To achieve customer satisfaction, the quality of our products and services must be our number one priority.
- *Customers are the focus of everything we do.* Our work must be done with our customers in mind, providing better products and services than our competition.

- *Continuous improvement is essential to our success.* We must strive for excellence in everything we do: in our products, in their safety and value — and in our services, our human relations, our competitiveness, and our profitability.
- *Employee involvement is our way of life.* We are a team. We must treat each other with trust and respect.
- *Dealers and suppliers are our partners.* The company must maintain mutually beneficial relationships with dealers, suppliers, and our other business associates.
- *Integrity is never compromised.* The conduct of our company worldwide must be pursued in a manner that is socially responsible and commands respect for its integrity and for its positive contributions to society. Our doors are open to men and women alike without discrimination and without regard to ethnic origin or personal beliefs.

Prior to our developing the Mission, Values, and Guiding Principles, quality was important but it wasn't discernably Ford's number one priority. It is now and has been for the past several years. At Ford, quality *is* job number one. Philip Caldwell, past chief executive officer of Ford, captured this idea in the following excerpt from his final address, "Preparing Ford for the Future":

> The first and overriding requirement is to get our quality right. It's always difficult at a time when you have to do many things to establish priorities, but the management of Ford deliberately put quality at the top of the list. The quality I'm talking about is not limited to products or, as a matter of fact, to our assembly plants and dealerships. Quality is an ethic, a course of action that governs everything we do.

We established the principles of striving for continuous improvement in every process in which we are involved so we will continuously satisfy customers' needs and expectations. We see our mission, values, and guiding principles as the capsule vision of the company we want to be.

We have developed a new policy statement which is a great departure from the way we've thought about quality in the past. Our policy is entitled *Ford Total Quality Excellence.* Let me describe what that phrase means.

Quality is providing products and services that meet customers' needs and expectations over their life cycle at a cost that represents customer value. *Total Quality* means bringing together the total effort of Ford, its supply base and the dealer organization, in achieving customer satisfaction. In a smaller sense it means the summation of continuous improvement of every process that ultimately adds to customer satisfaction. *Ford Total Quality* recognizes that our approach to quality is not generic nor academic. It builds on our Ford culture and heritage and meets Ford's unique needs. *Excellence* means being better than one's competition in attracting and satisfying the customer.

At Ford we now consider quality as customer-driven; quality is defined by our customers — they know it when they see it. We intend to pursue continuous improvements in every process, every system, in everything we do so that products and services of our company will truly excel in meeting customer needs and expectations.

What is Ford's definition of quality?

We define quality as "providing products and services that meet customers' needs and expectations, at costs that represent value to the customer." We recognize that you can't disassociate the customer value from other product satisfying attributes and customer expectations. That's why we've elected to describe it in this manner. It comes from the recognition that quality, productivity, and competitive position are inseparable.

Some people focus on reliability and do so by building redundant systems into their products. But the customer says, "That's not what I mean by a quality product because the added cost you've built in no longer makes your product a real value."

How did the improvement process get started?

It really got started when Henry Ford founded the company and established the objective of producing a car that would provide dependable personalized transportation for a price that most Americans could afford. A number of important events that have taken place since 1979 have greatly influenced our pursuance of never being satisfied with the status quo. To name a few:

- The tremendous losses of the entire U.S. auto industry and our own losses of several billion dollars in the early 1980s was a traumatic experience that demanded a deep soul-searching of every facet of our business.
- The dawning of understanding that the Japanese were for real in small car competition and would remain highly competitive in both quality and productivity.
- The introspective look we were forced to take at how our quality systems operated. In fact, all management systems had to be analyzed as to whether they were contributors or inhibitors to continuous improvement.

Can you expand on how your improvement process relates to all employees?

When we used to talk about quality we meant meeting engineering specifications. The focus was not on processes, but on the product. It left too many people out. In fact, an awful lot of people in the organization did not see how they could make a contribution to quality. That required redefining quality in customer terms and we've discussed that. For example, how can the accounts payable department have an impact on our customers? By improving the process, we reduce the cost of this function, and ultimately the products people buy from us can be a better value. We now believe that everything we do directly or indirectly impacts customer satisfaction. What we've done is said we wanted everyone involved in quality, in continuous improvement. Contrast that with an approach that describes quality as meeting engineering specifications. When all parts are generated within the specification, the work force has no further contribution it could make to quality. The quality goal has been achieved. However, we now understand that reducing variability and continuously improving cost effectiveness is the endless road to quality excellence. The concept opens up Pandora's box. Now we're never done. No one can ever say again, "I'd really like to be involved in continuous quality improvement, but what can I do?" We have completely redimensioned what we mean by continuous improvement in quality and productivity. The result will be *Ford Total Quality Excellence*.

When you talk about continuous improvement, does it apply in all areas or just the process areas?

We're convinced that everything can be looked at as a process. In any business, if we improve the process, we are going to have a better product at a lower cost to the consumer. Look at the automobile industry. In the early days, the work force was extremely heterogeneous. People from every country in the world poured into Detroit to find jobs. Few had much formal education and many did not speak English, thus creating a communication problem. What was done, as I see it, was to break down the manufacturing process into very small repeatable tasks. It worked pretty effectively, you've got to admit. We assumed that all employees worked to the best of their ability and that any mistakes would be caught by inspection.

Of course, inspection focused on defect detection. We tried to make sure that a bad product didn't get downstream (a bad product being defined as one that didn't meet engineering specifications). So if we saw that the product quality was deteriorating, there was a rapid response system — we put on more inspectors to cull the good from the bad. Well, when you stop to think about it, there is no conceivable way you're going to improve a product doing that. How are you going to have any impact on improving the process that generates the product?

We've begun to see the control of quality as a continuum. We see the focus of the control of quality going from defect detection through defect prevention and on to total quality — continuous improvement in all of our processes. That's the way we see the continuum at Ford. Of course, we have an internal system that assesses our products in customer terms. But continuous improvement in all of our processes — engineering, manufacturing, supply, purchasing, administration, marketing, sales, and service — is what *Ford Total Quality Excellence* is all about. The result, we predict, is products and services that better satisfy customers at better value.

What activities did you undertake to get started with your improvement process?

We asked ourselves, how did Ford grow? What made the company successful? It wasn't easy for us to come to grips with the fact that there was plenty of room for improvement. The trauma of the recession no doubt had a great deal to do with our willingness to recognize that some systems no longer served us as well as they had in the past. Then we were fortunate to get Dr. W. Edwards Deming as our principal consultant in the area of quality and productivity. Dr. Deming was the major catalyst. He became our mentor, our friend, and the burr under our saddle when we were off track or moving too slowly. He really started us thinking with questions like these: How do you define quality in your company? Are your products or services showing continuous improvement? What kind of a system are you using to control quality? Do you have an environment that encourages people to be meaningfully involved? How do you continually improve the process? Are slogans and motivational speeches the core of your quality effort? What tools do people need to meaningfully pursue quality improvement?

There's another important thing that happened. The company and the United Auto Workers Union agreed in 1978 that it was necessary to join forces and establish a national joint committee on employee involvement. The cooperation between the union and Ford blossomed into the most workable relationship I've seen in my 42 years at the company.

In the ensuing years, the union joined with the company and established an employee involvement process. We don't call it a program. We think of programs as ending and processes as never-ending. So we call it an employee involvement process. A principal focus for that process was improving quality, and all of our people could readily relate to it. Just as our principal statement says that the number one priority of Ford Motor Company is quality, the number one focus of our employee involvement has been quality.

This was the time Ford was facing some of its stiffest challenges. What do you see as Ford's greatest challenges today?

I'll once again quote from our annual report of 1984, which seems to say it so well:

> We're still not cost competitive with the Japanese. We require more hourly and salaried labor hours to make each car, and we pay more for each of those hours. Our quality, while greatly improved, needs to be even better. We're shooting at a moving target, as other manufacturers are trying to improve their quality also. We are committed to nothing less than continuous improvement in the quality of our products.

24

Can Ford be competitive in the small car market in the United States against the Japanese?

Donald E. Peterson, chairman of the board, responded to that very question. His response outlines what needs to be done:

> To achieve it, we must continue to become more efficient, to keep narrowing the hours-to-produce gap with Japanese-built cars, and to maintain the pace of improvements in manufacturing techniques and inventory control. The key ingredient is to make even better use of our people resources, and we are determined to do so.

When Ford started to implement the improvement process, did it run into any major roadblocks?

The bridges we used to go from a concept of defect detection to defect prevention and then to the concept of continuous improvement were not readily apparent. The systems' changes and the tools to progress have evolved over time and are still evolving. Convincing people in the organization that the company is truly willing to depart from the traditional ways of doing business, to find better ways, has been difficult.

Many companies have had problems convincing upper management that top management was serious about the improvement program/processes. Did you run into that type of bottleneck?

I think we were very fortunate in this company, because our senior management took the leadership. Our survival depended on it.

Do you have any estimate of what the cost impact is of the process you implemented? For example, how much did it save you last year?

When you improve the quality of products by over 50 percent in four years, you know that costs have improved significantly. Perhaps we put too much emphasis on trying to quantify the tangible cost improvement. What is the value of a satisfied customer over 20 years? What is owner loyalty worth? We are absolutely convinced that if you provide products and services that meet the customer's needs and expectations, at a cost that represents value to the customer, you will do it less expensively with quality as the focus than any other way. There is no doubt in my mind that improving quality in everything we do does not add to cost — it reduces cost.

Does the program really penetrate support areas like manufacturing, engineering, and accounts payable?

Well, when you talk about the transition and what's going on at Ford, the evolutionary process from defect detection to defect prevention, and then on to the concept of continuous improvement in every process, we've made good progress in our product areas. We are really just revving up to the idea of total quality excellence in the support areas. It's under way and beginning to expand rapidly.

Could you summarize the impact of the improvement program on your corporation?

I think the most important thing that has happened to this corporation is that quality has been declared the number one objective. It has given us a flag to rally around. There's a pride that's evolving in terms of measurable accomplishment — the fact that our customers are voting for us in the marketplace. There is a cohesiveness, a team spirit, that has resulted by focusing on quality as our number one priority.

Do you feel this impacts the workers on the floor?

Yes, tremendously. If you go to any plant and talk to our employees and ask them what the most important objective of the plant is, most would say that quality is their number one priority. They are not just saying it, they are living it.

What about suppliers? Have they too felt an effect from the improvement process at Ford?

Part of the story was printed in the annual report:

> Significantly, the company's 2,300 supplier sources doing business with North American Automotive Operations have made a commitment to excellence. In 1984, 109 supplier locations around the world were added to the 'Q1 Preferred Supplier Roll of Honor.' To qualify, a supplier must have an excellent quality rating and a well-developed and managed quality assurance system. In return, the supplier is given preferred status.

We have worked closely with our suppliers to help them understand how statistical thinking and process control can be applied to their environment. Many of them needed no introduction to the concept.

Did you use the improvement process as an awareness campaign or an educational campaign, and what was the overall effect?

We really did not know where we stood in relation to the competition. We had been very successful in America, and then the Japanese came over. Until we really studied that development in depth, we didn't know the degree to which we were at a disadvantage. The president of Ford decided that the company should retain Dr. Deming as a consultant. Some of the concepts we garnered by working with Dr. Deming were:

- Defect prevention versus defect detection.
- Customer quality through the life of the product.
- Continuous improvements in quality and productivity.
- The power of statistical thinking.
- Total quality that applies to everything we do.

We didn't conjure this up in those first few days with Dr. Deming. It took a long, long time to understand.

Donald Peterson summed it up at a meeting of our suppliers:

> The major factor in winning the battle against offshore competition will be our joint dedication to the concept of continuous improvement. In this effort, we march to one drummer. We're after the finest products in the world. No exceptions. And when we reach that pinnacle with your help, we'll aim for even better products so that no one can catch us. I want the drumbeat of continuous improvement to echo throughout Ford Motor Company operations — in every plant, in every office, in every laboratory, in every dealership.

(See Appendix I for more information on Ford Motor Company.)

General Motors Corporation

Corporate Background

General Motors celebrated its 75th anniversary on September 16, 1983. It was on this date in 1908 that William C. Durant founded the General Motors Company, predecessor of the current General Motors Corporation. The first company acquired by Durant was the Buick Motor Company. Within the next year, Durant added Oldsmobile, Cadillac, and Oakland (now Pontiac) to the GM family. The addition of a new automotive operating unit — Saturn — to GM's passenger car divisions was announced January 8, 1985. Saturn will add a sixth nameplate to GM's North American passenger car marques — Chevrolet, Pontiac, Oldsmobile, Buick, and Cadillac. Saturn is the first such nameplate added in the United States since Chevrolet joined the GM family in 1918.

Currently, GM has 151 facilities operating in 26 states and 90 cities in the United States and 13 plants in Canada. It has assembly, manufacturing, distribution, sales, or warehousing operations in 37 other countries. General Motors also has equity interest in associated companies which conduct assembly, manufacturing, or distribution operations in several countries.

Average worldwide employment totaled approximately 748,000 men and women in 1984. General Motors' principal products, besides passenger cars, include trucks, buses, locomotives, and a wide variety of other items for both commercial and defense applications.

Interview with F. James McDonald

President, General Motors Corporation

What were the circumstances leading to the current focus of GM on quality improvement?

The quest for quality has never been greater in the long history of our business. And it's fair to ask, "Why this sudden explosion of concern? What forces have moved quality to the center stage in my industry?" Was there a single event that forever altered our view of product quality? There were many. And they came together in the late 1970s, beginning with the Iranian oil cutoff and the sudden customer preference for fuel efficient cars. The demand for small cars, better fuel economy, and improved quality was almost immediate. Each of these market factors was cemented by the three-year economic recession which followed. And for some customers in this country, the Japanese seemed to offer the right answer to the changed circumstances in the marketplace.

Efficient, small, high quality vehicles from Japan and the availability of these vehicles at just the right time in history were watershed events in the U.S. auto industry. Their perceived quality became the benchmark for all cars — in effect, customer standards changed dramatically. And that change swept through the entire line of products.

This lesson of history cannot be ignored, and we at General Motors believe tomorrow's competitors will all be quality leaders — or they won't be in the picture at all.

Do you have an official quality policy?

Actually, the new quality consciousness at GM began with the development of a quality ethic for all GM units and operations. The essence of this ethic boils down to this: Quality is the number one operating priority at GM today.

What do you call your quality improvement activities?

We call it "quality improvement." But, I think it is important to emphasize that quality improvement isn't a separate activity at all — it's really a critical part of the entire management job. Until quality methods and attitudes become totally ingrained, I believe it will be necessary to continue to separately identify and stress the quality improvement process so that we can maximize results.

To what sections of the business is it being applied?

Quality improvement is being applied to all areas of our business. Specific quality objectives and strategies must be included within each unit's five-year business plan. All departments within a business, and of course each employee, contribute to meeting those quality objectives.

On new product programs, resources are allocated very early when our ability to influence the outcome is greatest. This includes the front loading of people from all disciplines including marketing, product engineering, manufacturing, assembly, quality assurance, financial, and materials management. This includes early sourcing decisions so our suppliers can work with product development teams on potential problems and improvements.

What activities were undertaken to start the quality improvement process, and when did it start?

Up to now, I've been using the word "quality" rather broadly. Of course, this word has a specific, as well as a general, meaning. And for those who work in the technology of quality assurance, the distinctions are important. But to capture the nature of the quality task, we've adopted a definition of quality which says simply this: "Quality is conformance to requirements and specifications which meet customer expectations."

As used in the broad sense at GM, quality includes features, functions, conformance, reliability, durability, performance, service, safety, and other characteristics which relate to high customer satisfaction. To carry out specific, measurable improvements, we have focused attention on four separate improvement criteria: quality, reliability, durability, and performance. All of GM's vehicle programs are being measured against these four criteria and their related subsidiary functions.

Proclamations on quality have little real merit unless they are coupled with the resolve and ability to put them into action. No real progress in quality and reliability is possible unless an organization shares a strategic vision of the task ahead. Without such a vision, neither resolve nor resources can be expected to produce much headway.

At GM today, we have this kind of strategic vision, and that vision is simply to offer world-class quality in every market segment. By world class, we mean parity with, or superiority to, the best in the field — product-for-product.

Such a goal requires use of all the classic quality forecasting and assurance technologies. It demands a clear understanding of where we are today, what the competitive demands will be in the future, and what we must do to earn world-class status. Each GM unit is now busy implementing a game plan, using typical apportionment techniques for major vehicle systems and the various subsections of the vehicle.

Also, working with local divisional people, a quality improvement plan and strategies are now being implemented at every operating unit of the organization.

To assist the operating units in this effort, the corporation has issued four key success factors for quality, which help focus the GM quality ethic and its six mandates. Research has shown that these key success factors must be addressed in business planning and implementation strategies if meaningful quality improvement is to occur.

Each key success factor is complemented by a series of objectives that should be reflected by all units of the organization as they continue to strengthen their quality improvement plans and implementation strategies.

31

Let's now take a look at what the key success factors and the associated objectives are.

Management commitment. Managers at all levels must be committed to continuous quality improvement and demonstrate their commitment by word and action.

Objectives:

- Make quality improvement the top priority in all business activities.
- Continuously manage and participate in quality improvement activities.
- Regularly communicate management's role in quality improvement and everybody's requirement to produce quality.
- Implement a systematic approach to quality improvement.
- Comprehend the philosophies of the classical quality approaches while being receptive to new quality ideas.

People development process. Every employee, regardless of function or level, must have the encouragement, support, and opportunity to be a contributing member of the quality improvement effort.

Objectives:

- Increase employee awareness and commitment to division and corporate quality improvement goals.
- Establish quality as a major component for measuring and rewarding people's performance.
- Equip every employee with the awareness, knowledge, and skill required to do the job right the first time.
- Provide the opportunity for employees to participate actively in quality problem identification and resolution.
- Build an organizational culture that results in openness, honesty, trust, and respect, and encourages responsibility and participation in continuous quality improvement.

Quality performance processes. Each task and activity must have processes and tools to ensure conformance to specifications and to provide for continuous quality improvement.

Objectives:

- Develop an implementation support tool, such as cost of quality, which estimates the cost of nonconformance and conformance.
- Use statistical methods to identify and continually reduce process variation.
- Establish cross-functional development teams to plan and implement preventive and corrective quality actions.

- Implement procedures to conduct root-cause analysis and implement irreversible corrective action against nonconformance.
- Establish supplier systems that ensure quality performance on a timely basis.
- Continually reassess requirements and specifications to ensure conformance to customer needs.

Customer satisfaction. General Motors must be the world leader in quality, reliability, durability, performance, service, and value, as confirmed by customer-defined measures and marketplace response.

Objectives:

- Develop appropriate short- and long-term measures to gauge success in meeting customer expectations.
- Use customer satisfaction requirements as the primary basis to evaluate programs, while including these requirements in the product design and build.
- Respond to the customer during the sales experience in a professional and trustworthy manner.
- Provide a high standard of service to meet customer's needs and requirements.
- Establish a responsive system for resolving customer complaints and problems in a prompt, customer-satisfying manner.

We have also identified the major steps to carry out improvements on any given project and have found that they work quite well:

- Establish the objectives: expected results, competitive assessment required, and management concurrence.
- Establish the method of measurement and its adequacy (predictive if possible).
- Identify the problems and rank order the opportunities for improvement (tests, field, and other).
- Determine the root causes of the problems.
- Determine and verify the changes to the product and process required to eliminate the root causes of the problems (irreversible corrective actions).
- Estimate the improvements from the changes and ensure that there are sufficient improvements to achieve objectives (competitive reassessment).
- Obtain concurrence by plant/division management for the improvements.
- Implement the improvements: begin on a current similar product or process to develop the experience and practice, practice, practice!
- Establish controls for the new level.
- Repeat the process.
- Implement the prevention process through the incorporation of findings and experience in new products and processes to prevent recurrence.

What is the role of top management in the improvement process?

To gain further insight into quality strategies at other companies in the United States, GM participated in a cross-industry visitation program in the fall of 1985. Members of our management spent time with their counterparts at 11 major companies — all well regarded for their outstanding quality programs. Not surprisingly, some of those companies are highlighted in this book, including IBM, Hewlett-Packard, and several others.

This study revealed that the most effective quality systems start at the top and that organizational achievement follows only after management commitment is in place. All the companies emphasized the need for a quality culture and ethic which transcends methods, products, or organizational systems. For example, in each company, customers really do come first. In each, production is controlled to produce quality. And in each, specific plans are in place, action systems are enforced, and total follow-through is a way of life.

I need not dwell further on these characteristics. Suffice it to say that doing things right the first time is part of the corporate woodwork at every company we visited. At GM we expect to gain much from this study, and I consider it one of our wisest investments.

Achieving true quality maturity is totally the responsibility of top management in our company. Others may carry it out to one degree or another, but those at the top must be willing to go the whole route.

We believe that the whole top management team must be aboard. Even the most inspiring leader can't hope to reach the organization without total commitment from everyone at the top. Total quality demands total attack. There is no room for mixed messages or polite indifference. Despite what some writers have said, I do not believe that quality arises as a natural event within large organizations. In fact, crosscurrents and separation of interests can hardly be avoided in big organizations. And these are natural breeding grounds of resistance when it comes to making fundamental changes. Only constant effort and slavish follow-up can help avoid these potential potholes — and that's especially true in quality and reliability.

Phil Crosby has pointed out that people perform to the standards of their leaders. If management thinks people don't care, it's likely that people won't care. But, far more important, if people think that management doesn't care, it's almost certain that no one else will either.

What is the role of the employee and the union in the improvement process?

We are absolutely convinced that eventual success depends heavily on the employees. As we discussed, one of our key success factors for quality improvement concerns people development processes.

Many studies have pointed out that technical tools, professional quality systems, and management leadership are vital to any lasting success. But these same studies make it clear that willing employees who are trained and trusted can create a competitive edge in every quality effort — regardless of the product or location.

We are making headway on employee involvement at almost 100 GM plants. These programs are separate from specific quality and productivity activities. But we've found again and again that improvements in the quality of an employee's work life pay direct dividends in virtually every other area of concern — including the quality of the product.

For instance, we've trained more than 30,000 GM workers in statistical process control (SPC) techniques. And I must say, to see these tools put to work right on the line is one of the most rewarding experiences I've had at GM. So, I think we're on the right track on the employee side — even though we still have a ways to go.

Also, joint studies are being conducted with the United Auto Workers Union to implement improvements. An example is our new automotive operating unit, Saturn, created to produce small cars in the United States that are competitive in all aspects with the lowest priced imports. Saturn's operations will be greatly influenced by concepts developed by the GM-UAW Saturn Study Center.

What problems did you have in implementing the improvement process?

We're now in a sort of middle ground on the quality cycle. Currently, techniques such as SPC at the point of manufacture are providing outstanding improvement, as verified by the more recent new products. Statistical techniques are helping to ensure that the process is being controlled. The whole focus must be on process control, not inspection of the parts.

But prevention within manufacturing can take you only so far along the journey. Greater success must come from moving the focus upstream to design and engineering, for example, by combining the talents of design engineering, processing, and manufacturing, and having them work together as a team instead of individually. That's the place to start if you're serious about doing everything right the first time. Our product development teams on new products that we previously mentioned are addressing this in a fine manner. We are also initiating this concept in our daily operations.

GM's reorganization of its North American passenger car and its worldwide truck and bus operations addressed changes necessary to ensure quality improvements, accountability for results, and effective allocation of resources. The reorganization was quality-driven from the beginning.

Another challenge was to convince management that conformance to requirements would result in continuous product, productivity, and schedule improvement.

Also, we must constantly remember that in organizations with sound objectives, most people do what they think the organization wants them to do. So signals are very important.

I think we overemphasize the so-called resistance of middle management. In a large company you have to expect a variety of change rates. In fact, at GM we recognize that some middle managers are well ahead of their bosses and the employees who work for them. In those cases where middle management *is* lagging, you still can't escape the simple fact that top management is ultimately responsible. Managers have to go home at night and look in the mirror and answer the question, "Did what I've said and done today reinforce the quality ethic or not?" That's the acid test, and every manager along the line has to pass it.

What has been the impact on the support areas?

As we have mentioned, we have reorganized our operations to focus our efforts better on satisfying our customers. Within these reorganized units, a team approach using all disciplines and our suppliers is proving to be quite effective in meeting our objectives. I believe we are seeing a greater, more consistent personal commitment to quality than perhaps at any time in our history. We are also seeing a much greater involvement of the people in our support groups in making this happen.

Do you have a cost of quality system?

Many of our units have cost of quality systems. We see this as a tool to support quality improvement. Also, we do know that the money categorized as quality costs is huge and that the cost portion related to nonconformance to specifications is a significant source of funds to justify needed quality improvements.

Can we discuss some specific examples of improved performance?

We are pleased with the things that are happening in our new product development. The key to our approach is product development teams. These teams involve the right mix of people up front, starting prior to prototype design. It is an effort with individuals from all disciplines including engineering, manufacturing, service, assembly, material management, financial, and quality assurance.

As an example, one such effort concerned the engine mounting system for a vehicle to be introduced several years from now. This system has to be world class when the vehicle is brought to market. The challenge of identifying what is world class led to the creation of the Mona Lisa process. The Mona Lisa process was devised to serve as a tool for competitive vehicle assessment. The name Mona Lisa was chosen because most people would relate it to world class. What makes it world class is its harmonization of features and not one thing in particular. The "best" cars in the world were acquired for the Mona Lisa display and are assessed for their competitive advantages in overall car, features, quality, and functions categories.

The Mona Lisa process uses two assessment techniques through which world-class features are identified.

One technique involves the disassembly of parts of various GM and competitive vehicles to the nut-and-bolt level to enable a part comparison. These disassembled parts are on display at the Mona Lisa for team members to analyze for differences. This vehicle teardown is also beneficial in evaluating the manufacturing and assembly processes.

Another technique used as an assessment tool is the test driving of competitive vehicles by team members. The vehicles can be signed out for a short period of time to be test driven or driven by a group in a comparison ride. The individual driving the vehicle is requested to complete a survey that contains questions geared toward the driver's perception of vehicle characteristics. In other words, sight, sound, touch, and feel characteristics are distinguished for the best-in-class products. These become the minimum design objectives for a new vehicle and become integrated into a total vehicle that is better than the current best-in-class vehicle.

The Mona Lisa process aided the product development team in identifying how the engine-mount system has to be designed to be world-class.

The product development team selected the world-class suppliers for their parts early-on. These suppliers joined the team and aided significantly in the new design.

For example, the number of parts in the system was reduced by over one-half from that in the current vehicle that it replaces. This not only improved buildability, but promised greater reliability as well.

A supplier with a long-term commitment was able to make substantial investment in improved processing and now forecasts significant decreases in quality costs.

All of this was possible before prototype design releases. This is where the real payoff has to be.

We are also pleased with what is happening in our improvement of existing products through root-cause analysis. Root-cause analysis operates on the premises that there is a fundamental reason why something occurs and that all problems can be prevented.

If we know why the problem happened, an irreversible corrective action can prevent it from recurring. That is the key to thorough root-cause analysis. You know you've done your job when you can turn the problem on or off by applying or removing the solution. To make this work we can no longer believe that in any human endeavor errors are bound to happen and you have to live with them. Also, you can't believe that perfection in a product or service is not economically feasible. Root-cause analysis denies both of those myths.

Take the case of the keys that would not unlock the doors on a series of GM cars. Through field and in-plant reports, the problem was found to occur only in two-door models. Yet, sedans used a similar door-lock mechanism. Typical thinking might have led to the redesign of the door lock for both sedans and coupes when the series was revamped — probably in six years. In the meantime, all coupes would have been inspected and faulty ones would have been fixed — a costly venture. And even with a new design and tooling change, no one would have understood why the problem happened in the first place.

Using root-cause analysis, it was discovered that a retainer clip for the lock mechanism loosened during the door glass installation — an assembly procedure that differed slightly on two-door models. It took close tracking of more than 1,000 vehicles, trips to suppliers, and a selling job to plant management. But when the process was finished, an immediate corrective action was put into place, and work began to redesign the retainer clip for coupe models. Total cost to track the problem and implement a solution was $5,000. Had the problem run its course through the life cycle of the series, the estimated cost of in-plant and warranty claims alone would have been $1.3 million. And that doesn't take into account the number of potentially dissatisfied GM customers. With the new clip design and the understanding of why it loosened, the problem can be prevented in all future GM models, which is really where the big payoff occurs.

Avon Products, Inc.

Corporate Background

Avon Products, Inc., is a multinational, multibillion dollar company with headquarters in New York City. Its Avon Division, which contributed 81 percent of corporate consolidated sales in 1985, is the world's foremost manufacturer and distributor of cosmetics, fragrances, toiletries, fashion jewelry, and gift and decorative products. Its diverse operations also include Avon Direct Response (direct mail businesses of wearing apparel for women, men, and children) and Foster Medical and the Mediplex Group Inc. (two health care services companies).

The Avon Division markets its products worldwide. More than 1.3 million Avon Representatives sold Avon products in 1985 through a direct selling method that goes back to the company's beginnings. This marketing technique provides personal service in the customer's home and encourages the development of a trust and friendship between the Avon Representative and the person to whom she sells.

In 1985 the Avon Division had an operating profit of $234.6 million on sales of $2 billion.

Interview with James E. Preston
President, Avon Division

Does the Avon Division have an official quality policy?

The Division's quality policy, which I signed in May 1984, reaffirms the principles that have guided our company since it was founded. We have always been committed to serving families throughout the world with the highest quality products backed by a guarantee of satisfaction. We believe that inferior quality tarnishes our reputation and jeopardizes the relationship between a Representative and her customer. We consider that relationship to be the most important of all, because it is the foundation on which our company was built.

Because we drew up our quality policy as the charter for our Quality and Productivity Improvement Process, many hands participated in its preparation and many revisions were necessary before the final version was issued. The policy clearly defines the specific actions required of Avon employees at all levels and all over the world. It has also been translated into the languages of our international companies.

We consider it important enough to present a copy to every graduate of our Quality Education Seminars. And we reinforce it through special video presentations, newsletters, and other forms of employee communication.

This is the way it reads:

Quality Policy, Avon Division

The principles that guide Avon require that we always provide products and services of the highest quality.

> We cannot stint on quality. Whatever carries the Avon name must reflect the highest standards of purity and safety. It must be pleasing to look at and, above all, it must work the way we say it will.

To ensure that this principle is maintained, it is the policy of the Avon Division to strive for excellence in the products and services that we provide to our customers and Representatives. In doing so, we will strengthen our position of leadership in quality and our reputation for fully meeting the needs and expectations of our consumers.

In order to meet all specified and implied standards of performance, every Avon location and function will carefully plan and do the following:

- Set specific requirements for everything they do.
- Define quality as conformance to the requirements.
- Constantly measure quality and reduce their own cost of not meeting the requirements.
- Give our customers, Representatives, and each other defect-free products that work the first time, every time.
- Support, educate, and expect each other to make quality first among the equals of quality, cost, and service.
- Instill a genuine commitment to quality and excellence in all employees.

Corporate success depends on our individual and collective contributions and commitments to this quality of performance.

What prompted your company to reassess its quality effort?

It was a question of dollars and "sense." Money was being spent that should have been saved. We also were faced with the challenges of a changing marketplace, both at home and abroad.

We recognized that, despite our traditional dedication to quality standards, lapses in quality were costing us money and customers. Because we have a money-back guarantee, customers return products they aren't completely satisfied with. Returns were costing us money. And that's only part of the loss. A disappointed customer isn't as likely to buy from us again. We had no way of knowing what *that* was costing us, but it was probably plenty.

We also realized that we had been achieving the good quality of our products by inspection — that is, by finding defects and culling them out. The costs of quality inspections and of other accounts, such as spoilage, rejected materials, and material usage variations, were all incurred because of failure to "get it right the first time." An analysis in the United States of these accounts revealed to us that nonconformance to measurable quality standards in our products and services was costing the Avon Division tens of millions of dollars annually. To be able to eliminate that cost through an effective quality management program was an opportunity we jumped at.

How did the quality process get started?

Having identified the problem, we established a task force, headed by Hans Zimmer, director, Quality and Productivity Improvement, to attack it. To gather the facts it needed, the team looked at the quality programs and policies of IBM, J.P. Stevens, General Electric, NCR, 3M, Westinghouse, and Celanese.

The task force researched the works of well-known consultants in the field. Among them were W. Edwards Deming, whose successful crusade for quality and productivity helped turn Japanese industry around in the 1950s; Joseph Juran, whose emphasis in Japan was on massive programs of education for management and the entire workforce; and Philip Crosby, who simplified the highly technical theories to make them acceptable to broad segments of American industry. Crosby's 14-step process emphasizes the importance of management initiative in controlling the "cost of quality" and in establishing "zero defects" as a performance standard.

The task force examined the Japanese experience with quality circles and how that concept had worked — or not worked — in companies outside Japan.

After all the concepts had been considered in light of the Avon experience, the task force recommended integrated quality management — the forerunner of our Quality and Productivity Improvement Process.

Integrated quality management would enable us to reduce costs and increase productivity. It would improve quality and give us a vital strategic weapon in the battle for market share. And it would assure a price/value relationship for our products that would appeal to our customers.

41

The task force defined IQM as a prevention-oriented process for which every Avon manager, employee, and supplier would be responsible. Its rallying cry would be: "Do it right the first time." Failure to do it right would run counter to our fundamental corporate objectives of guaranteed customer satisfaction and return on investment.

By November 1982 all three of our U.S. laboratories were using IQM. Europe became the first major international area to initiate the program, and Latin America followed in May 1983. Recognizing that the IQM program might be viewed as a short-term initiative, the task force recommended that it become known as the Quality and Productivity Improvement Process, or QPIP.

Since QPIP drew substantially on the theories of Philip Crosby and Associates (supplemented by concepts from other experts in the field), we dealt with the Crosby organization in a consultant capacity. After an exploratory visit and in preparation of the QPIP strategy, we sent 125 senior management employees to PCA seminars in Winter Park, Florida, and Tarrytown, New York. I also attended a special one-day session.

Immediate reactions were mixed, and we realized the necessity of modifying some of Crosby's generic concepts to suit our specific needs. However, it soon became clear to the majority of participants that in the area of quality management, they had not been doing as well as they had thought.

An integrated quality process was a revolutionary concept in our functionally oriented environment. Individual departments had always pursued their vested interests and operated within their own departmental budgets. Rewards were given for quantity of output (despite rejects), for handling crises, and for adherence to schedules, rather than for solving problems and seeking causes so as to prevent problems from recurring. Traditionally, responsibility for quality and for implementing quality programs rested with the quality departments.

Were there any problems in implementing the process?

A lot of thinking had to be turned around. Most people had never been given a clear definition of quality, nor the guidelines for achieving it. And if the cost of quality was defined as the cost of nonconformance to customer requirements for safe, functional, effective products, nobody was quite sure how to determine when quality was improving and when it was not. Where quality assurance had previously exercised control by inspection, using reject and defect levels as measurements, now every individual would be involved in building quality into the product.

Primary resistance came from entrenched, successful areas where managers were accustomed to a certain amount of built-in waste and processing spoilage. Their focus had always been on meeting efficiency requirements and quotas.

Their crisis-ridden, tight schedules discouraged prevention procedures. Many viewed QPIP as "just another program that would disappear if it were quietly ignored." They also rejected the idea that it could be applied successfully beyond the manufacturing environment.

It was also difficult to generate interest in the process itself. The concepts seemed too basic. Most people believed that paying attention to quality was nothing new but was something they had always been doing. They perceived the process to be additional work. Attitudes ranged from "What's in it for me?" to "I've got problems of my own and other jobs to get done."

We needed to overcome several misconceptions. One was that quality improvement is limited to products; the next, as I mentioned before, was that quality improvement is just another program; another was that quality is the responsibility of the quality department; and yet another was that the process should be implemented by the quality department.

We had to refocus the culture and philosophy of our company. We had to initiate a broad educational program that would improve comprehension, change attitudes, and decentralize responsibilities. Projects for quality improvement would, from now on, cross departmental lines.

We had to make people aware of the ripple effect of imperfect planning — the unforeseen errors, overtime work, extra materials, squeezed schedules, and omitted final checks that result in a failed product. The quality department would clarify quality expectations and provide the tools and the training, but the responsibility for quality would belong to everyone. And, from the top down, everyone had a special role to play.

How would you describe your company's quality improvement program?

We think of QPIP as a process because it is never-ending and because it involves all of us — at all levels and in all functions. However, it starts with management's understanding of and commitment to the four absolutes of quality:
1. The definition of quality is conformance to requirements.
2. The approach to achieving quality is prevention.
3. The quality performance standard is zero defects.
4. The measurement of quality is the price of nonconformance.

We also recognized that the improvement process could function effectively only with full management support. Exposure to Crosby's concepts at the executive college sessions had convinced our officers of the tie between quality and productivity improvement. We no longer had any doubt that effective quality management would help us to reduce costs and increase profits.

Many of Crosby's basic principles are found in our QPIP in one form or another. Among them are assigning a price tag to nonconformance, emphasizing involvement throughout the company, and setting a goal of zero defects. However, we modified the terminology, the formulas for calculation, and the roles and responsiblities to conform to the Avon environment. We refined Crosby's 14-step procedure into Avon's Nine Points which became the essential elements in our improvement process. Let's take them point by point.

We've talked about management commitment. That's the first and most critical element. Second, we established an organization. In each area we formed a Quality Council made up of the general manager or a senior executive and selected members of his management staff. The Quality Councils guide and manage the improvement process and encourage the free flow of communication to and from the improvement teams. These teams consist of employees from all levels who meet to work on specific project assignments. We rely on them to identify opportunities for improvement, resolve problems, and put their resolutions into effect.

The improvement teams are supported by *ad hoc* committees assigned to plan and coordinate specific tasks related to the improvement process, such as measurements, cost of quality, systems for corrective action, employee communication, recognition, and so on.

Our third point is to generate the enthusiasm and sense of involvement that keeps our improvement process moving forward. To do this we use newsletter articles, posters, contests, and audiovisual presentations. We also hold employee meetings to discuss specific improvement activities, recognize achievements, and encourage awareness of further improvement opportunities.

Our fourth point, which is vital to the success of the process, is training and education for employees. People need to understand our quality philosophy. We teach measurement and management of quality by emphasizing improvement through defect prevention and permanent elimination of the causes of defects.

Our Quality Education Seminars give our employees the knowledge and common language they need to carry out their roles in the improvement process. Built around the idea of avoiding problems before they occur, these seminars provide employees with basic quality principles, a problem-solving process, and better insight into the identification of quality opportunities that exist within their jobs.

These seminars really work. Here are comments from some of our first-line supervisors who participated.

From a closing and dock supervisor:

> The training made me sit down and think how we are doing things and how we can do them better. I learned how to measure so we could see how we

are performing in the first place. I've not only established requirements, but I now have a measurement system in place. The training sessions broadened my mind. I now think of what really causes problems instead of just applying a bandage approach all the time.

From a branch management associate in information systems:

Quality training has raised my awareness of the implications of quality and how nonconformance can turn into dollars, and, therefore, have a negative impact on the company. The Quality Education Seminars have encouraged me to spend more time up front and save a lot more time in the end. I now plan more and do more preventive-type things up front. I try to troubleshoot before any problem occurs so as not to ruin a software program and have to correct the program after the fact.

From an operations manager in personnel:

It really makes us refocus our attention as to what the requirements are and what we want to get out of a job. Requirements are the same as expectations — so we can more clearly define what our expectations are to our employees.

Our quality training programs draw on many resources. Our methods development group provides the tools for analyzing process flows, challenging existing operating methods, and developing new ones by applying principles of motion economy.

Safety resources training makes people aware of the impact of accidents on productivity and provides an understanding of the principles of job safety analysis and safety performance accountability.

Sales exposure brings employees closer to the customer and the Representative to raise the level of concern for their needs.

Our special skills training programs are designed for specific functions and levels within the company. Communication workshops teach the use of visual aids and help participants organize material and hone the skills they need for making presentations.

We also provide team leadership training that concentrates on the effective functioning of teams with members drawn from many disciplines. Sessions include brainstorming, storyboarding, and problem-solving techniques.

Our fifth point concerns the development and implementation of a quality plan. In this plan we identify key quality issues and determine issue objectives, requirements, measurements, action plans, and intermediate goals.

Sixth, we calculate the cost of quality — not only to determine the price of nonconformance but also to measure progress and establish improvement priorities. To do this calculation we adapted Crosby's formula:

Total operating costs = PONC + POC + CODB

The price of nonconformance (PONC) is the cost of not conforming to requirements, that is, the cost we incur for any loss of resources due to defects, errors, failures, etc. The price of conformance (POC) is the cost for obtaining conformance through appraisal and/or inspection and prevention. The costs of doing business (CODB) are the valid operating costs incurred in running the business without making any defects or errors, or incurring any failures.

After all these activities are well under way, we initiate a formal system to generate and process requests for corrective action or recommendations for improvements. For actual or potential nonconformance situations, we assign improvement teams to identify causes and to eliminate them permanently. To generate the improvement recommendations, we define projects and then assign teams to analyze, evaluate, and challenge current activities. Then these teams develop and implement ideas for improvement.

The eighth point in our improvement process is recognition. To sustain team participation and involvement, we have established a system for rewarding high performers. Sometimes the acknowledgment is individual, and sometimes it takes the form of group recognition for sustained effort. We try to make sure that the reward is personal and tangible. The recipient or recipients are determined by our Quality Councils and by peer groups or support teams.

The last of Avon's Nine Points relates to supplier quality. We establish supplier requirements in terms of contract specifications, making sure that requirements, methods, and policies are mutually acceptable. Then we set standards for supplier evaluation and selection based on performance capabilities and future potential. We also have a supplier corrective-action system to follow up on nonconformances. Our supplier quality training program is an extension of the Quality Education Seminars. The more dependable our suppliers become, the less we must spend on inspections, processing rejects, culling defects, or shipping replacement components.

A supervisor in our data processing department captured the attitude of employees toward our improvement process:

> We're trying to get back to what I believe the company used to be quite a few years ago, when we cared more about quality. I think the idea that this isn't going to happen overnight, that this is a process and a journey, is very positive, because I think it will be done that way when everybody is contributing to it.

Understanding that quality and productivity improvement is a process and a journey, rather than a destination, is the key to success. In a presentation introducing the concept to the division's international companies, I remember Hans Zimmer saying that quality improvement is a long-term, evolutionary process, requiring time, perseverance, and continual fine tuning. It's a process that aims to do nothing less than change the basic attitudes of every employee at every level. We want to instill in ourselves and in our employees a genuine caring to do things right the first time, to promote involvement and teamwork so we can pool our ideas in the search for better solutions.

What are the roles and responsibilities of the participants in the process?

We established specific responsibilities for each participant in the process — manager, customer, supplier, company, individual, and quality improvement team.

The manager's role is to set an example, educate, organize, support, and encourage the quality improvement teams, and, generally, to participate in quality improvement efforts.

In the context of QPIP, we use the terms "customer" and "supplier" internally to refer to anyone who receives the output of someone else or provides a product or service to another. In these roles, customers and suppliers are asked to establish mutually agreed upon requirements which can be met 100 percent of the time. We hold the customer responsible for giving measurable feedback, following up on nonconformances, and listening to the supplier's suggestions.

The company itself is responsible for providing the necessary resources (both personnel and money) to establish the Quality Council and to implement the quality plan.

The role of the individual is to support the process, suggest improvements, participate on the improvement team, and adopt zero defects as a performance standard.

Finally, the role of the quality improvement team is to analyze problems, report progress to the Quality Council, eliminate nonconformances, issue a final report, formalize the corrective action, and ensure follow-up.

What quality measurements were developed to evaluate progress?

Once we had defined the requirements, roles, and responsibilities related to the process clearly, we established measurements to identify nonconformances and track progress in eliminating them.

One of our teams of experts built an input/output model that tracks conformance to requirements in every step of our production process. The model starts with the supplier of raw materials (because what goes in often determines what comes out) and continues all the way to the customer who buys the finished product. The model is a useful tool that helps us define requirements for a new process, clarify requirements for an existing process, or improve a process or situation where we are encountering problems.

Another research group developed a closed-loop problem solving process, which is continuous until the misstep that's creating the problem is eliminated permanently. There are five levels in the closed-loop process:

1. We define the nonconformance.
2. If necessary, we temporarily fix the nonconformance to keep the business going.
3. We examine the causes of the problem.
4. We take specific corrective actions to eliminate each cause.
5. Finally, we evaluate and follow up to find out whether the corrective actions are working. If they're not, then we redefine the nonconformances and start the process all over again.

We measure on an ongoing basis to correct the nonconformances before they show up in the final product — a proactive, rather than a reactive approach.

We generally try to attack major areas that typically reflect the cost of "doing it wrong." In processing, these might be rejected or reworked batches or microbiological rejects; in packaging — line rejects, poor setups, or defective components; and at the distribution level — rejected or reconditioned finished goods or customer returns. At headquarters, examples of doing it wrong include lateness, change, or cancellations affecting the product delivery systems, print service errors, and imperfect control and administration of sales materials.

In the product delivery system, for example, some of the areas in which we measure quality include:

- The timeliness of design turnovers.
- The specificity of package profiles.
- The accuracy of cost sheets/quotes.

These are all repetitive processes that have value-added activities and input and output that are measurable. The measurements are internal and tell us how well the product is meeting the division's requirements.

After the product is delivered, we use external quality measurements to determine if it meets customer needs and specifications. This requires:

- An understanding of customer expectations.
- The quantifying of customer experience information.
- The development of quality indices to measure and track quality performance.
- Effective communications.
- Procedures for taking corrective action and following up to make sure the action is successful.

Communication is especially important, because the key to good quality measurement is feedback. We must have a constant incoming and outgoing flow of information — accurate and systematic surveys, analyses, and reports — at all levels and from all sources.

How was the process phased into Avon Division's operations?

We decided to introduce QPIP into all areas of the company gradually, with operations designated as the first phase. We formed a Quality Council in operations to initiate the process worldwide in manufacturing, shipping, distribution, and delivery.

In April 1983 we selected a manufacturing/distribution facility in Morton Grove, Illinois, to test the program. We formed support teams and improvement teams to ferret out problems and determine the cost of quality. We set up education seminars for all employees and generated the spirit and enthusiasm for "doing it right the first time." We prepared an operations manual that has since been modified and used in other areas. And we appointed a "Beacon"— a sort of ombudsman of quality — to serve as a driving force and to keep the process on target.

The pilot program was successful and clearly demonstrated the potential of QPIP as a company-wide, prevention-oriented quality effort. Training of Beacons and instructors in other operations areas began in the late summer of 1983.

We produced two videotapes which were used as resources for the initial Quality Education Seminars. The first, *Right From the Beginning*, focuses on the Avon philosophy: To produce products people need with the quality they can trust, and to do it right from the beginning.

Using Avon employees as spokespeople, the film stresses our traditional commitment to scientific quality — the purity, safety, and effectiveness of our products. It also describes the rigorous microbiological, toxicological, and pharmacological testing and chemical evaluation each product and formula undergoes. The best ideas, the videotape points out, come from a continual effort to outdo what has already been done by ourselves and others and to do it better than ever before.

The second tape, *The Concepts of Quality Management*, is an introduction to quality improvement training that discusses what quality is and how to manage it. It identifies the four absolutes of quality management. And it establishes clearly that the cost of building quality into the product is five percent of sales, while the cost of nonconformance is 20 percent.

The first phase of the process is virtually complete, although, in fact, QPIP is never finished.

Early attempts to move into the second phase — that is, to introduce QPIP into our New York headquarters environment — met with resistance. The time requirements were unacceptable, and there were too many levels of interpretation of important issues. Crosby's generic approach required adaptation to our needs. So it was back to the drawing board to make the necessary revisions. It is important to remember that in pursuing our quality improvement goals we are constantly reexamining our materials and our methods. Departmental instructors are now trained by the quality department not only to apply the generic concepts, but also to relate them specifically to the needs of their individual departments so as to gain more immediate and wholehearted acceptance.

Having made the necessary adjustments, we began the second phase, the implementation of the process in marketing and administration with the formation of the Marketing Operations Quality Council and other headquarters councils and the training of support teams. Quality education instructor training followed, and by the spring of 1985, 96 beacons/instructors had been trained in Quality Education Seminars and 2,470 Avon employees had attended the seminar, including 1,212 headquarters employees.

The third phase, initiated by the group vice president of sales and her officers, extends the quality management process into the sales environment.

What are some of the future plans and goals for the process?

Our future plans and goals for quality and productivity improvement call for continued expansion. Our first priority is the further development, analysis, and enhancement of quality systems for headquarters, manufacturing, and distribution locations. Our emphasis will be on the importance of measurement systems as the best way to identify nonconformances and to track progress in their elimination.

We will streamline our quality systems to reduce the number of "how to" steps and concentrate on defining critical activities, roles, and responsibilities. We will introduce greater flexibility within the procedures to improve efficiency.

In the near term, we will initiate quality education in each sales area and in the headquarters sales support group. And we will establish quality measurement systems within employee sales centers to provide accurate and timely feedback on product quality.

Fully implemented, we expect QPIP to be an integral part of the Avon culture. It will become a way of life for every employee — exempt and nonexempt, white collar and blue collar, in the laboratory and at the desk, in every area of the company — international and domestic, manufacturing and non-manufacturing, service and sales.

How have you determined the cost of quality?

Last year we spent about $300,000 on education and the implementation of QPIP, but we recorded savings totaling more than $10 million, all directly attributable to QPIP.

We now have ongoing price of nonconformance reporting. This year, we formed a Headquarters Cost of Quality Team, with two key management employees from our controller's department as cochairpersons. The objectives were to:

- Identify areas of nonconformance in all major business segments in Avon Division's U.S. operations.
- Assist functional departments in developing a cost of quality reporting system.
- Provide progress updates to the Quality Council.
- Develop a consolidated quarterly cost of quality report.
- Review on an ongoing basis departmental systems and procedures to identify potential problem areas.

Our next steps are to:

- Review areas of 100 percent nonconformance in functional areas.
- Develop strategies to control and reduce costs.
- Provide the Quality Council with updates on the status of quality improvement team initiatives.

What are some of the results?

Through April of 1985, we achieved a reduction in our targeted nonconformance accounts of 35.5 percent from the prior year.

Notable among examples of improved performance are two headquarters departments, which together achieved savings of $2.5 million as a result of applying the quality principles of QPIP.

Bill Saunders, manager of purchase order development in our print services department, addressed the problem of purchase order print errors and late and inaccurate inputs that can affect thousands of Representatives in every campaign. He was able to obtain error-free performance for seven consecutive campaigns in the third year of his action plan. Less vendor overtime and increased order processing efficiency at the branch level resulted in an annual reduction in the price of nonconformance of nearly $500,000 annually.

Alvor Brown, manager of literature estimating and trending, concentrated on reducing excess brochures. The number of brochures left unused at the end of 1983 amounted to 34.3 million and cost the company $3.8 million — enough pages to cover Central Park in New York 10 times over. Brown was able to reduce the excess from the average of 1.3 million per campaign in 1983 to .6 thousand in 1984, and even further to .4 thus far in 1985. This adds up to a savings of $2.4 million over two years.

These two key successes alone are an impressive record. (See Appendix II for more details.)

What was the impact of QPIP in the support areas of the company?

Participation in QPIP has heightened the awareness of our support groups that the services they provide are an essential part of a continuous process. They have begun to recognize that nonconformance to service specifications can result in delivery of a nonconforming product.

By assigning specific quality functions to every department, we have made self-evaluation and identification of profit opportunities a matter of personal pride.

Even our creative groups now realize that the quality improvement process has a positive effect on creative output. By spending more time "up front" and asking the probing questions necessary to establish mutually agreed on design requirements, they can eliminate the need for going "back to the drawing board" because of misunderstandings.

We recently restructured our marketing department, and as a result, it is now responsible for managing every step in the process of bringing a product to market. This will help us ensure that the quality, image, and value of our product line meet customer needs.

How would you summarize the impact on the company overall?

Recognition of the profit opportunities that were missed by "not doing it right the first time" has effected changes in our corporate culture. Our management emphasis now is on long-term plans and strategies that will bring about quality improvement in all work areas. From the top level down, roles and responsibilities have been changed and redirected, and resources have been committed in support of the integrated quality effort.

Everyone now speaks the common language of quality improvement — the four absolutes, cost of quality, corrective action, nonconformances, zero defects, and other dedicated terminology.

With better use of resources and higher operation profit, the Avon Division will be able to maintain a leadership position in its markets and assure greater employment security for its employees.

In the areas of the company where QPIP is in full-scale operation, the results speak for themselves: more uniform quality output, fewer errors, less rework, on-time completion, more efficient use of resources, reduced idle time, and less unproductive effort. Prevention really does mean control of the process.

Quality at Avon has become a way of life.

Corning Glass Works

Corporate Background

Corning Glass Works is a worldwide organization with $1.9 billion in annual sales, supplying more than 60,000 different products a year to some 47,000 customer firms and millions of individual customers. Corning operates 45 plants worldwide and has equity interests in some 21 affiliated companies.

Corning competes in the following four broad sectors:

- Specialty glass and ceramics (e.g., TV bulbs, ceramic products, technical glassware, and materials).
- Consumer housewares (e.g., dinnerware, ovenware, bakeware, and giftware).
- Laboratory sciences (e.g., laboratory glassware, medical diagnostic instruments, clinical testing services, and optical and ophthalmic products).
- Telecommunications (e.g., electronic components, and optical waveguide fiber and cable).

Interview with James R. Houghton
Chairman and Chief Executive Officer

Do you have an official quality policy?

Yes, we do. After I formally announced that the company was going to undertake a major, long-term effort to improve the quality of the firm's products, services, and management transactions, the management committee and I developed not only a quality policy, but a quality goal as well.

Our quality policy is simply this:

It is the policy of Corning Glass Works to achieve total quality performance in meeting the requirements of external and internal customers. Total quality performance means understanding who the customer is, what the requirements are, and meeting those requirements, without error, on time, every time.

Our quality goal is to make Corning Glass Works a leader in delivering error-free products and services, on time, that meet the customer requirements 100 percent of the time.

What do you call your quality improvement activities?

When we decided to make Corning a total quality company, we did a lot of searching to find an approach that seemed right for Corning. Eventually we settled on Phil Crosby's basic tenets, described in his book, *Quality Is Free.*

We tailored that approach to Corning's culture and arrived at what we call our Quality Management System. That system consists of four principles and 10 actions. The principles are:

- Meet the requirements.
- Error-free work.
- Manage by prevention.
- Measure by cost of quality.

The 10 actions are:

- Commitment
- Education
- Teams
- Measure/display
- Cost of quality
- Communication
- Corrective action
- Recognition
- Event
- Goals

When did it start?

Officially, it all began in October of 1983 when we announced to the company that we were going to make quality and profitability the two main objectives of Corning Glass Works — and to do that, we were going to become a total quality company.

Unofficially, it started five or six years ago at local unit level sales and manufacturing organizations, and was a response to a couple of emerging pressures. The first pressure was from our customers and our competition. More and more, quality was becoming a major requirement. In some cases it was as important as or even more important than price. And of course, we felt Japan's influence in a big way. While our quality record over the years was very good, and perceived as such by our customers, we were seeing a new standard.

We simply had to get better faster, or not survive as the kind of company we are today.

The second pressure was an internal one and came from our employees. Although they said it in many different ways, the message was always the same. They saw better ways of doing things, and they wanted to participate in the process of implementing those better ways.

Improved costs were also a factor, but in the beginning I must admit very few of us really believed improved quality meant lower unit cost.

To which sections of the business is it being applied?

Every single one. Achieving total quality requires commitment, participation, training, and enthusiasm at *all* levels of the company. We're a diverse, multinational company, with 45 manufacturing locations and 49 sales or service locations in North America, Europe, Latin America, and Asia-Pacific. Our products range from Pyrex bakeware and Steuben crystal, to ceramic substrates for catalytic converters, lighting products, medical instruments and testing services, optical and ophthalmic products, fiber optics, spacecraft and aircraft windows — I could go on, but the point is that each individual in every business, and at every level, is contributing to the success of this quality effort.

What activities were undertaken to start the improvement process?

I was elected chairman in April of 1983 and spent the next six months with my new management committee deciding how we would run the company and make the tough decisions that the coming years would require.

One major decision was to pursue total quality and make it part of everything we do. We announced this to the company and followed up with several key decisions. We appointed as director of quality a distinguished general manager and former board of directors member who had headed our international business for years. We then asked our three product line groups and two staff groups to appoint their own quality executives. These people formed our Quality Council which, in turn, was charged with the task of finding and implementing the process by which we would pursue total quality. Our people recommended, and we agreed, that our approach would be based on Crosby's basic ideas, adapted to Corning Glass Works.

Our first educational task was to provide total quality awareness training to all employees worldwide. This required development of a theology, curriculum, faculty, facilities, and management. Our audience consists of more than 27,000 employees in North America, Europe, Latin America, and Asia-Pacific. We had to communicate this message in American, Japanese, French, Spanish, English, German, and Portuguese.

We established a specially dedicated Quality Institute and built a new training facility in Corning, New York, to house it. We staffed the Institute with 10 full-time instructors in the United States and six instructors offshore. We established a Quality Council with representatives from all the major Corning units. Total quality for the company was identified graphically by a distinctive logo — our quality apple — which subsequently became quite important as a unifying factor that needed no translation.

We developed a three-day course for quality improvement teams and a two-day course for all other salaried employees. Curriculum development turned out to be an intensive process. It took four months and involved the resources of our professional education staff and Quality Council members, and time with outside consultants. Textbooks were developed, using Corning case histories as examples.

In communicating our quality policy, the first step was to start persuading our people that quality is important, that better ways of operating are possible, that we were going to find those ways, that we needed their help, and that we were in this for the long haul.

We built a structure for quality and set guidelines for teams throughout the company. The management committee (comprised of the six top corporate managers) sets quality policy, authorizes resources, reviews results, and leads and supports the company.

The corporate Quality Council, which I mentioned briefly before, includes representatives of each product line and staff group plus functional leaders, and converts policy into corporate-wide activities. The Council also looks outside for examples of quality efforts in other companies with whom we can share information.

Division-level steering committees for both product line and staff divisions set direction for each division, and establish tone and expectations for those divisions.

Quality improvement teams, or local unit teams, manage the quality process at the unit level. Corrective action teams and quality circles, then, actually *make* the improvements for which we are searching.

What problems did you have in implementing it?

Our problems revolved around four questions that were being asked from the boardroom to the factory floor. Those questions were:
- Aren't we already a quality company?
- Why do we need more quality?
- How do we get it?
- How will we pay for it?

Our initial problems centered on changing the way people thought about quality and how they thought about the way they worked. The key for us was introducing the concept that each of us has "customers" — inside our offices and our departments as well as across the company and outside the company — and those customers have requirements that must be met. This was a new and tough idea for many of us at first. But people were quick to grasp the usefulness of this concept, and the need, after we made the competitive picture clear. I must say that the whole concept of quality has gained almost universal acceptance throughout the company. It appeals to everyone's desire to do a good job, to do things right the first time. The problems of actually *making* quality improvements are going to be with us for some time, however.

How did your upper management become involved?

Corning's upper management has been involved from the very beginning. In fact, two vice chairmen, three group presidents, and I attended the company's first Quality Institute seminar held over a weekend in January of 1984.

If total quality is to become a way of life here at Corning, and I'm certain that it will, it's important that all employees understand that the commitment comes from the very top. Commitment from all of the members of the Management Committee is probably the single most powerful factor in consistent, uncompromising leadership to the organization — and even then, it will take some time to convince all of the people that we are serious.

Can you estimate what it cost to implement the process and what savings you realized last year?

We have not tracked savings on a corporate basis. Part of the change we require at Corning is to *not* manage this effort in the conventional way, with financial reports, savings estimates, and the like. We're putting our emphasis on *achieving* quality, and many times this requires more of a hands-on, walk-around-the-floor approach.

As for cost, in the first 15 months we spent, on a corporate out-of-pocket basis, about $1 million — mainly for education, instructors, materials, facilities, and consultants. And we expect an ongoing rate of $2 to $3 million per year at the corporate level. Of course, when we go into the product line and staff divisions, costs are greater, and if we include all the people time, costs are substantial.

What has been the impact on the support areas?

Support, or staff, areas have been a real challenge. The manufacturing areas, of course, have several advantages: They have physical products, a documented process, established measurements, and a department with a sign on the door that says "Quality." For many manufacturing areas, it is a case of doing the same things better than they did before.

Staff areas, on the other hand, often have to start from "ground zero." Some of them are still figuring out who their customers are. One of the reasons it's difficult is that they are dealing with issues of judgment rather than things you can count. But we're encouraging *everyone* to look at their work as a process. The point is that *all* work can be clearly defined in terms of inputs, outputs, and process steps, including work done by the support groups. Once this is done, it's much easier to apply Total Quality and see where improvements can be made. Some staff groups are making dramatic progress. Over time I am sure they'll all be on track, but there's no denying that it's tough.

Do you have a cost of quality system, and if you do, what impact did the improvement process have on reducing cost of quality?

We've always been involved with cost reduction and containment of one form or another, but the Quality Management System helps us to focus on cost of quality as we've never done before. Now it's one of our 10 action steps. We estimate that Corning's cost of quality is approximately 30 percent of sales — and that figure is typical of most U.S. companies. At Corning, cost of quality is being used to identify opportunities, to help prioritize those opportunities, and to set targets and measure progress. It's a tremendous tool, but we are taking great care to ensure that it is not used as a club. Cost of quality must be understood as a tool for local use.

Can we discuss some specific examples of improved performance? I would like examples that cover both manufacturing and the support areas, if possible.

One of our more notable successes has been with the automobile catalytic converter business. About three years after we invented the product, built a factory, and started shipping to Detroit, the Japanese arrived with a similar product that was so competitive we were faced with losing the business. With a determined plant manager, training, employee participation, and a lot of hard work, we regained our position. The plant is now shipping at a parts per million level we thought impossible just a couple of years ago. Incidentally, this plant now exports *into* Japan.

In the United Kingdom a new consumer product was gaining excellent acceptance in the marketplace. Even though the sales and marketing team felt confident about their position, they followed the Quality Management System and conducted an in-depth analysis of two things: their customers' requirements, and how well those customers thought their requirements were being met.

To their surprise the team learned that while people loved the product, many did not think highly of Corning's sales and service actions. In fact, some customers were having a tough time entering orders. Today, a large effort is underway to ensure all the customers' requirements are met, all the time.

Other examples range all the way from making it easier for everyone in an office to access needed forms to equipment improvements that have saved thousands of dollars. We have much larger examples, and many smaller ones, but the point to remember is that it's not size that counts. We are more interested in everyone working on quality in a quality way every day. It all counts, and at Corning we're making quality work.

How would you summarize the impact the improvement program has had upon your corporation?

I think we are experiencing the most dramatic change in the company's history. Right now, most of that change exists in the minds of the employees. They know a new direction is required. They know that top management has established the way this new direction will take place. They understand that the competition is getting a lot tougher. They know they can make a much more significant contribution through personal participation. I guess the best way to sum it all up would be to say that it is a good start on a very long journey.

General Dynamics Corporation

Corporate Background

As a leading defense contractor in the United States, General Dynamics develops and produces advanced weapons systems for use on land, sea, and in the air. The application of high technology also characterizes its major commercial products — space launch vehicles, advanced information systems, and commercial aircraft subassemblies. Its commercial activities also include coal mining and the production of lime, concrete, and other construction materials.

General Dynamics comprises 15 major divisions and subsidiaries and has annual sales of more than $8.9 billion. It has 104,000 employees, of whom more than 12,400 are scientists and engineers. They work in 48 states and 45 foreign countries. General Dynamics' headquarters is located in St. Louis, Missouri.

The company is deeply involved in five vital and separate fields — aerospace and electronics technology, shipbuilding, military land systems, natural resources and construction materials, and general aviation aircraft.

General Dynamics' aerospace divisions produce the F-16 Falcon multimission jet fighter, the Tomahawk sea-launched and ground-launched cruise missiles, the Atlas and Centaur launch vehicles for defense and commercial missions, the Phalanx shipboard gun defense system, a range of air-to-air and surface-to-air missile systems, defense and space electronics, radar systems, and fuselages and engine struts for commercial jetliners.

Shipbuilding activities encompass the design and construction of giant nuclear-powered Trident ballistic missile submarines, the construction of high-speed, fast-attack submarines, and design and construction of maritime prepositioning ships for America's Rapid Deployment Force.

Military land systems activities include production of the M1 main battle tank for the U.S. Army and the M60 main battle tank for the United States and foreign countries.

General aviation aircraft involvement began in 1985 with the acquisition of Cessna Aircraft.

Interview with Oliver C. Boileau
President, General Dynamics Corporation

Do you have an official quality policy?

Yes we do. The current corporate quality policy was published on February 4, 1981, and covers three points:

- It is General Dynamics' policy to provide products and services commensurate with the standards demanded by our customers. It is the division general manager's responsibility to establish and maintain sound, cost-effective quality practices in his or her division.
- Each general manager will be held accountable for obtaining the requisite quality and for ensuring that proper actions are taken in engineering, manufacturing, materials, and quality assurance. All other functions also share in the responsibility to deliver quality products and services.
- General Dynamics recognizes the vital importance of its product and services in our national economy and defense and that of our foreign customers. This policy will not be compromised.

What do you call your quality improvement activities?

We call it the Productivity/Quality Improvement Process (P/QIP). We have structured the process to address effectiveness and efficiency of any function. A QIP measure is established to grade the effectiveness of each process we wish to improve, such as reducing the number of engineering errors in the design drawing system. Then we establish one or more productivity improvement projects (PIP) to improve the efficiency of the design release system, such as the Electrical Harness Data System project which reduces aircraft electrical harness and component design time and drawing errors, thus reducing production flow time, scrap, rework, and repair.

When did it start?

We have always placed heavy emphasis on quality and have been in the forefront of Department of Defense efforts to improve quality. Our people in the four aerospace divisions have been highly instrumental in helping the Department of Defense write such quality specifications as MIL-Q-9858A, MIL-STD-1520, and MIL-STD-1535. We also assisted in developing the recent DOD/Defense Industries Quality Excellence Program. In addition, part of our corporate strategic planning took several steps in 1980 toward institutionalization of the process: (1) we established a Corporate Vice President for Productivity and Quality, (2) we issued the Quality Policy, (3) we established a Steering Committee of Division Vice Presidents of Production and Quality Assurance, (4) we established a task group to develop some corporate common QIP parameters, and (5) we launched the formal process in mid 1982. Our P/QIP served as a model for the Aeronautical Systems Division Quality Improvement Strategy and the Air Force Systems Command Functional Management Review programs. P/QIP has evolved into our GD 2000 program which features coordinated top management support of product supportability, quality, schedule, and cost.

To what sections of the business is it being applied?

Originally, the formal corporate program addressed the general manager, engineering, program offices, production, quality assurance, logistics/field service, and procurement/material. It is, however, being progressively applied to all functional areas.

The corporate common QIP parameters are listed as follows:

Organizational Measures and Goals
(Corporate: Common Elements)

Organization	Measurement Parameter
Engineering	Avoidable changes per month
Program Office	Deviations/waivers
Materials	On-time deliveries to production
	Accepted purchased items
Production	Scrap (labor)
	Scrap (material)
	Rework and repair
	First time yield
Data Systems Center	Software change requests
Quality Assurance	Inspection escapes
	MRB QARs per 1,000 direct labor hours
Logistics	Service report response time
General Manager	Overtime

Subsequently, the program was applied to all functions at the division levels. There are as many as 60 QIP parameters and hundreds of projects in PIP. Each general manager is measured on P/QIP results, and he, in turn, measures his staff on P/QIP accomplishments. One division's QIP parameters at the end of 1986 are shown in Figure 1.

Quality Improvement

I. GENERAL MANAGER

Divisional Overtime

II. FINANCE

III. CONTRACTS

Proposal Responsiveness | Invoice Collections
Journal Voucher Errors

ICAP Deficiency Reports

VI. F-16 PROGRAM OFFICE

Deviations/Waivers

Operational Readiness
Class I Changes
Operational Reliability
Operational Maintainability

V. PRODUCTION OPERATIONS

Yield
Scrap
Rework/Repair

Facilitization
Overtime

IV. HUMAN RESOURCES

Grievance Activity
Employee Requisition Activity
Exempt Employee Training
Personnel Change Processing
Health Claims Error Ratio

VII. QUALITY ASSURANCE

MRB QAR Frequency
Inspection Escapes

DD 250 Errors
Overtime
Supplier Inspection Escapes
Material Survey Activity
ZD Aircraft Deliveries

VIII. ELECTRONIC FABRICATION CENTER

Yield
Scrap
Rework/Repair
Overtime

Corporate Common Param

Division Unique Paramete

X. RESEARCH & ENGINEERING

Avoidable Engineering Drawing Changes

IX. LOGISTICS

Service Report Response Time

Tech Order Error Rate
Spares Schedule Performance
Support Equipment Schedule Performance
Mod Kit Schedule Performance
Spares/Support Equipment Acceptance Rate
Mod Kit Acceptance
Overtime

QAR Costs
QARs per Ship Set
Avoidable OFP Software Changes
Service Report Response
Liaison Request Turnaround
Overtime

XI. DATA SYSTEMS CENTRAL CENTE

On-Line IMS Abnormal Terminations
Batch Production System Abnormal Terminations
Quality of Deliverable Software
Labor Hours to Correct CADAM/Computervision
Errors/Deficiencies

XII. MATERIALS

On-Time Deliveries to Production
Accepted Purchased Items

Inventory Control
Overtime

Figure 1

64

What activities were undertaken to start the improvement process?

As discussed previously, we started with a strategy in 1980. The formal process with the divisions started on September 18, 1982, using the Juran Institute and the top quality gurus of the U.S. Air Force, Army, and Navy. Dr. Juran, Jack Lavery, Sy Lorber, and Will Willoughby presented a two-day seminar to 118 top executives of the Corporate Headquarters and the Aerospace Group of Fort Worth, Convair, Pomona, and Electronics Divisions. We followed this with Juran seminars for all management/supervision at each division. We sent over 3,000 managers/supervisors through the initial seminars. We presently are using in-house developed programs supplemented with video programs from Juran, Deming, and Crosby.

What problems did you have in implementing it?

We had no major problems. Several of our divisions already had management systems that addressed most of the 13 corporate common elements. There were the normal everyday problems of middle management resistance, some changing of standard definitions for some of the elements — such as total labor hours or just direct labor hours as a base for some parameters — and some divisions had to make minor modifications to their Management Information Systems tracking system to collect the required data.

How did your upper management become involved?

Top management saw the need for a quality/productivity revolution as part of our corporate strategy and so initiated the process. Top management created it, tracks it, and runs it, and we are seeing impressive results both internally and externally by our customers' use of the products.

Can you estimate what it cost to implement the process and what savings you realized?

This is most difficult to answer because we did not use dollars as a measuring criteria; however, we did spend approximately $400,000 in the implementation training. We consider this process part of our normal operating mode, so the costs are not broken out. Two of our divisions do cost out the savings from QIP. For instance, the Fort Worth Division had savings of $43. 8 million for 1983/1984 (Figure 2). You might note that they did not achieve all their aggressive goals, so dollars were subtracted under delivery of materials to production from the suppliers.

Fort Worth Division
Quality Improvement Program
Corporate Common Parameters
Cost Savings versus 1982 Baseline Data

Function	Element	—1983— $ Savings	—1984— $ Savings	Program $ Savings
General Manager	Overtime reduction	13,965,255	3,165,721	17,130,976
Engineering	Avoidable engineering changes	3,601,360	17,462,396	21,063,756
Program Office	Deviation waivers per aircraft	798,560	823,200	1,621,760
Production	First time yield	172,415	180,155	352,570
Production	Direct labor hours for scrap	202,051	(1,859)	200,192
Production	Value of raw material scrap	294,340	176,237	470,577
Production	Direct labor hours for rework/repair	1,339,881	583,201	1,923,082
Material	Production material on-time delivery	(57,016)	(1,360,708)	(1,417,724)
Material	Purchase item acceptability	70,401	204,223	274,624
Logistics	Service report response time	52,752	68,283	121,035
Quality Assurance	Rejection reports for material review action	464,821	1,349,770	1,814,591
Quality Assurance	Nonconforming items which escape planned inspections	(55,451)	275,943	220,492
QIP Grand Total Savings		$20,849,369	$22,926,562	$43,775,931

What has been the impact on the support areas?

They have been very supportive of the original program because they could see the tangible benefits coming from the factory, engineering, and field support. Schedules were easier to meet; thus, cash flow for finance improved. Scrap, rework, and repair went down and factory yields went up, helping us to meet or underrun contract costs, so the contracts department was elated about meeting the negotiated rates, etc. But the white-collar and support departments being actively measured and tracked under the P/QIP process is the other half of the question. Approximately 60 to 70 percent of our work force is now "non-touch" (i.e., white-collar) labor, so the mid-range part of our P/QIP strategy was to get all the departments into the process. As I mentioned earlier, the divisions are now tracking QIP parameters and PIP projects in finance, contracts, human resources, and data services. We have a special department at corporate and division levels working on improving the white-collar work force. We are actively working with the American Productivity Center on six projects in the white-collar area. These white-collar studies, measurements, and techniques will be added to the P/QIP process and applied throughout the corporation.

Do you have a cost of quality system and, if you do, what impact did the improvement process have on reducing cost of quality?

Yes we do. We regularly report these figures to the Aerospace Industries Association Resource Study. We use these statistical data for internal division management. The P/QIP process revolution has given us some impressive results. My performance objectives to the divisions for 1985 were:

- *Quality.* Establish 30 percent better improvement goals than that of 1984 in QIP. Establish zero discrepancy goals as a percent of total units delivered or total systems incorporated by the customer.
- *Productivity.* Track the corporate productivity measures and establish challenging goals.
- *Schedule.* All programs must be on or ahead of contract schedule by mid-1985.
- *Personnel.* Design and implement training and development systems to improve P/QIP with a goal of 20 hours per exempt employee.
- *Capital facilities.* Productivity/quality improvement methods, systems, and processes will be emphasized.

This type of company emphasis is reducing our nonconformance costs in all areas. The attitudes in all functional areas are showing improvement, and we have quality improvement task teams working to raise quality in all departments.

Can we discuss some specific examples of improved performance? I would like examples that cover both manufacturing and the support areas, if possible.

The bottom line on our program process or revolution is meeting the quality performance, cost, and schedule requirements of the customer. Several of our divisions are showing dramatic improvements in both cost and schedules, which are the direct result of quality work and attitudes. Some specific results are:

- *M1 tank.* The U.S. Army has designated our Lima, Ohio, facility to be used as a quality assurance training facility (as a *quality* model) for other Army plants and contractors. Since we purchased this division in 1982, we have decreased rework hours by 73.1 percent, are achieving an all-time high of 95 percent first time yield on all our machined parts, up from 89 percent two years earlier, and delivered our first Zero Discrepancy M1 Tank to the Army in 1984. We are ahead of our QIP goal on ZD deliveries. The weapon system is performing very well in the field, having won its last two operational readiness competitions against other countries.

- *F-16.* The Fort Worth Division has excelled in the quality arena. Their pursuit of improving quality has improved the manufacturing nonconformance costs from 7.9 percent of direct labor hours in 1980 to 3.3 percent in 1984. This is a saving of $37 million. The F-16 ZD delivery performance is reaching an all-time high of 84 percent and for three consecutive months it was at 100 percent. For the customer, the F-16 weapon system operational readiness rate of 87.7 percent (June 1985) is outstanding, and all other performance measures established by the U.S. Air Force for the operational F-16 are being exceeded. All these systems have been delivered on or ahead of schedule, and the program is under target cost.

- *Stinger/Post.* The Pomona Division was the recipient of the 1985 Certificate of Merit PAT (Productivity through Assembly Technology) Award by Assembly Engineering Magazine. The award was given for outstanding achievement in productivity through assembly technology related to our electro/optical assembly center project. The center is in the process of being installed and will be used to assemble bulkhead subassemblies for Stinger/Post weapons.

- *Missile programs.* The P/QIP process has really impacted the engineering design release system at our Convair Division. The number of errors made on drawings released to the manufacturing line decreased from 41 percent in 1981 to 11 percent in 1985. Design it right the first time to build it right — that is our motto.

How would you summarize the impact the improvement program has had on your corporation?

It's working the way we intended! We had some dramatic results because we assigned very tough (20 to 50 percent) improvement goals. We institutionalized the process and are continually looking for ways to improve and add to it. We are aggressively working the office, technical, and support areas; we are using all available resources to get a handle on this 60 to 70 percent of the workforce.

We have special activities going on with our supplier base, because 50 to 60 percent of our systems are purchased. We are working P/QIP with our suppliers and overseas co-producers. We are equally weighing quality, technical competence, cost, and schedule performance in our source selection.

The revolution is working, but it will not be completed until we get each department and each person to rededicate their efforts to quality "ownership!"

AT&T

Corporate Background

AT&T, a global provider of telecommunications services and equipment, is in the business of meeting customer needs for the electronic movement and management of information throughout the world. The company had operating revenues of $34 billion in 1986 and total assets of $39 billion. It employs more than 300,000 people.

AT&T provides a broad range of telecommunications and related services. These include network systems for telecommunications companies and governments worldwide; domestic and worldwide long-distance services for resident, business, and government customers; private branch exchanges (PBXs) and computers for businesses of all sizes; electronic components; telephones and other related products and services for consumers; and special systems for the federal government.

Although AT&T traces its beginnings back to 1885, it is in many ways a new company. With the divestiture of the Bell operating companies from the parent corporation in January 1984, AT&T left a long era of protected monopoly to compete in the telecommunications and computer markets. While this change has imposed many new requirements on the corporation and its people, it also carried forward many traditions that continue to serve it well. One of those traditions is an emphasis on quality.

Interview with Eugene J. Eckel
The following interview was conducted while Mr. Eckel was vice president, Manufacturing — Switching Equipment in AT&T's Network Systems Group. He is now president and chief executive officer of AT&T and Philips Telecommunications.

Do you have an official quality policy?

Yes. Our policy makes it clear that we do not consider quality management a discipline apart from others or the responsibility of any one group. It makes

71

quality an integral part of every facet of our business and an important aspect of everyone's job.

The policy also acknowledges that quality is a necessary condition of customer satisfaction. It pledges us to provide products and services that meet customers' expectations, and to pursue programs that make every employee an advocate for the practitioner of quality.

The policy, endorsed by AT&T chairman James Olson, commits us to provide quality while meeting all schedule and cost objectives. It also focuses our efforts on processes and procedures essential to high quality.

When did these activities start?

AT&T pioneered quality improvement in the 1920s and 1930s. But more recently we've reexamined and reemphasized quality as the nature of our business has changed. For example, the Bell operating companies, which used to be part of the corporate family, are now independent entities, and that's made a difference in how we deliver quality to them. Of course, we also have customers we didn't have prior to divestiture.

New standards of quality are emerging on a global scale, and we must be able to meet them. At the same time the company's technology base is changing. In software or semiconductor products, you cannot see problems after a product has been made. So you must determine quality in new ways. And, of course, evolving technology has provided us with new tools for focusing on quality — computer-based tools that can help us plan manufacturing resources, design for manufacturability, and so forth.

To which sections of the business is it being applied?

We're integrating quality improvement across the business. Starting with the president of AT&T and down through the company's various business units, organizations have been formed to address the issue of quality improvement. In AT&T's Network Systems Group, they've formed a quality council composed of every vice president in the organization, plus three from the appropriate areas of AT&T Bell Laboratories. Its mission is to provide the leadership and direction to a quality improvement process which spans and connects every phase of our business operations.

In a sense, however, these groups are only the tip of the iceberg. The issue of quality is permeating the entire organization. In Network Systems, for example, quality begins in the marketplace, with market analysis and product planning, and ends in the marketplace, with customer feedback. And it suffuses all the steps in between — product and process design, and production and distribution, to name a few.

What activities were undertaken to start the improvement process?

Several task forces have been formed to address the major quality improvement thrusts. These task forces constitute a multidisciplinary approach to a number of quality improvement projects affecting everyone.

Additionally, top management has thrown its support behind training in quality at all levels, the zero defects concept, and application of scientific tools and processes. Our upper-level managers also have supported methods of measuring customer satisfaction with our programs.

What problems did you have in implementing the process?

The biggest problem has been in realizing quality gains where people traditionally have not considered themselves directly involved with quality — the so-called white collar areas. When an ordering clerk misses a quantity by an order of magnitude, that error can result in materials shortages on the factory floor. And the engineer who doesn't do his or her process engineering carefully, resulting in yields of 92 percent instead of 98 percent, affects the profitability of a product.

The point, of course, is that quality is everyone's job. What we're striving for is a change in the corporate culture — the values virtually everyone embraces — that will integrate concern for quality into all jobs.

How did your upper management become involved?

As I mentioned, upper management was supportive in many ways. They got so involved because we could demonstrate the financial ramifications of good quality and bad. They saw that high quality and low cost, far from being mutually exclusive, were inextricably linked.

Can you estimate what it cost to implement the process and what savings you have realized?

It's difficult to tell exactly how much the quality improvement process cost, but I do know it's only a fraction of the savings realized. In Network Systems, for example, we realized measurable quality-related cost savings of $150 million in 1985.

What has been the impact on support areas?

There's been a noticeable impact on the areas that immediately support the manufacturing process. For example, we know that the accuracy in our storerooms has improved. That's important because you can't run a line efficiently if the storeroom doesn't provide you with the right materials or is slow in getting the materials to you.

In one storeroom, for example, after carrying out a number of quality studies and acting on the results, accuracy of orders delivered increased more than four times. One of the things those studies revealed was that a large percentage of the employees working in the storerooms needed additional training to do their jobs. So we organized the appropriate classes.

More studies revealed that weigh scales used to measure quantities of small items sometimes were placed beneath blowers that ventilate the storeroom. The pressure from those blowers threw off the scale readings, so we moved the instruments to a place where they wouldn't be affected.

The process goes on and on. This case is not only a good illustration of how a continuing quality study affects support functions, but of how an aggressive quality effort can change the whole character of an operation.

Do you have a cost of quality system and, if you do, what impact did the improvement process have on reducing cost of quality?

Yes. It addresses three elements in the cost of quality — prevention costs, failure costs, and appraisal costs. Our experience is that the first costs to come down with the introduction of quality improvement are failure costs. Then, as product quality continues to improve, inspection costs start to shrink as quality gains continue. At the same time, the investment in prevention will increase, although the overall costs will be reduced.

Our cost system is how we arrived at the $150 million-plus savings for 1985.

Do you have some specific examples of improved performance, especially in the manufacturing and support areas?

I refer you to the case history that follows. It's a look at some effective quality improvement efforts at our Oklahoma City Works (see Appendix III).

How would you summarize the impact the improvement program has had on your corporation?

It has proven itself a necessity for financial success.

Hewlett-Packard Company

Corporate Background

Hewlett-Packard Company is an international manufacturer of measurement and computation products and systems used in industry, business, engineering, computation, medicine, and education. The company employs 82,000 people worldwide and had revenues in its 1986 fiscal year of $7.10 billion.

Interview with John Young
President

Do you have an official quality policy?

I'd say the most official recognition of quality's strategic importance can be found in Hewlett-Packard's corporate objectives, which form the basic framework or constitution for the company. The goal is "...to provide products and services of the highest quality and greatest possible value to our customers, thereby gaining and holding their respect and loyalty." That makes quality a goal in every business activity we undertake.

What do you call your quality improvement activities?

We don't have a special name for them, because we don't view them as some unique "pet" program that's isolated from the mainstream of our daily activities. We're trying to institutionalize quality — to make "doing it right the first time" something we do as a matter of course.

When did it start?

Hewlett-Packard products have always had a pretty enviable reputation for quality, but our view of what that meant changed quite radically back in 1979. At that time we did an internal survey of our manufacturing costs. That study revealed that fully 25 percent of our manufacturing assets were tied up in reacting to bad quality — to finding and fixing problems. So I announced what we call a "stretch" objective for the 1980s — a 90 percent reduction in field failure rates. We've since announced a similar goal for software quality. But this time we'll try to achieve it in five years.

To which sections of the business is it being applied?

It applies to every aspect of our business. Total quality control is a discipline that forces you to look at every activity as a process that can be defined, measured, and improved.

Of course, we began our quality efforts in manufacturing because that was familiar territory where results could easily be measured. But we've since taken the same methodology and applied it to order processing, marketing, R&D, personnel — everywhere.

What activities were undertaken to start the improvement process?

Let me answer that question two ways, and you can take your choice as to which answer you're looking for.

Historically, to start our quality improvement process, we sent a small group of leading manufacturing managers to Japan. We have a joint venture there — Yokogowa-Hewlett-Packard — and it won the coveted Deming Prize for quality a couple of years ago.

So our people came back from Japan all fired up, and they started quality projects. Then a little healthy peer competition helped keep the momentum going, with each division trying to outdo the others in quality improvement. Of course, Hewlett-Packard's a pretty yeasty environment, and the total quality control process fit in well with our approach to management and the way we use our own information technology internally. So, with the challenge from me and the results from some leading-edge divisions, we got the thing rolling.

Now for a second way to answer your question. If you mean the exact process steps (like Crosby's) through which we kick things off, it begins with identifying the customer and his or her expectations and needs. Then we select an issue related to those needs, map out our process for satisfying them, decide what performance measure we'll use, and then decide what data should be collected and where and how we should gather it. Once it has been collected, we analyze the data and decide how to implement improvements. I'm sure I may have left out some of the intermediate steps — we have quite a well-defined set of them — but you get the idea. It's an analytical methodology that fits in well with the kinds of people you find in a measurement computation company like Hewlett-Packard.

What problems did you have in implementing it?

Implementing quality programs has been no problem at Hewlett-Packard. The bigger challenge has been to institutionalize it. It's easy for a manager to focus on other goals — getting shipments out the door, for example. Encouraging people to pursue quality as *the* strategic goal requires some changes in attitude. Quality efforts that cross departmental or divisional boundaries are essential but difficult, and that fact has led us to constantly reevaluate our organizational structure and performance measurements.

How did your upper management become involved?

We were involved from the start. My "factor-of-ten" improvement challenge is one example. Other members of our executive committee have been strong champions. Whenever we review a division's performance, quality is one of the areas where we want to see results. I suppose another signal of upper management support is the fact that we recently moved the corporate quality department and made it report to our chief operating officer — a move we hope will highlight the broad relevance of total quality control to all our activities and management's emphasis on it.

Can you estimate what it cost to implement the process and what savings you realized over the years?

We never thought to quantify costs, because satisfying customers — the basic goal of total quality control — is a very necessary cost of doing business.

Savings are much easier to quantify, though I suppose it's difficult to isolate quality improvements as the only factor affecting these ratios. However, improved quality is one of the prime reasons we've been able to reduce our inventory so significantly, since now we don't need the "margin of error" we used to need. In 1979, when I stated our quality goal, Hewlett-Packard's inventory ran at about 20.5 percent of sales. Last year it was under 14 percent. You multiply those ratios out and you have a savings of $475 million.

When we applied total quality control to our order processing function and improved the quality of information in our invoices, the result was a reduction in accounts receivable. That has saved us about $151 million over the past seven years.

I could go on with other examples, but you'd run out of patience listening to them.

What has been the impact on support areas?

By "support" do you mean support people or after-sales support? Let me just cite one example that shows the impact both ways.

Our United Kingdom distribution center was responsible for sending out parts and supplies to Hewlett-Packard customers. Employees there were under a lot of stress, and the group worked an average of 600 hours of overtime monthly. The problem was the month-end bulge, when more than 25 percent of their total shipping was done in the last three days of the month. Even with temporary help they still felt like they were always playing catch-up.

So they formed a total quality control team and did a process flow chart for their activity. When they'd done it, they saw that the process was unnecessarily complex. So they simplified it, and in the year since they made the changes, productivity is up 68 percent. And they're able to accommodate the same amount of work with half the number of people.

I like that example — and it's just one among many small improvements like it — because it shows how that clerk in shipping and receiving can use total quality to have a positive effect on his or her own job. People like doing good work, and the total quality control methodology provides them a way to do it.

Do you have a cost of quality system and, if you do, what impact did the improvement process have on reducing the cost of quality?

We don't have a formal, company-wide system per se, but we do collect data in an aggregate form from many of our divisions to help measure our progress. Many entities routinely collect their costs and use them to identify opportunities and measure progress.

Can we discuss some specific examples of improved performance? I would like some examples that cover both manufacturing and support areas, if possible.

I've mentioned some specifics already, but let me briefly cite a couple more. One example in manufacturing is a quality project in our Avondale Division, where manufacturing and R&D people formed a team at the very beginning of the project. The result was a new gas chromatograph that used 75 percent fewer parts, cost half as much to manufacture, was five times as reliable, and required a tenth of the floor space to manufacture. I might add that, even though it's technologically superior to its predecessor, it sells for 25 percent less.

On the support side, here in the United States, repair turnaround time is down 20 percent in the last year alone. The number of repairs that technicians or service people can complete on their first attempt has increased six-fold because of better availability and quality of repair parts.

How would you summarize the impact the improvement program has had on your corporation?

It's given us a common conceptual framework — the ability to view our activities as processes, to agree on measures of success, and to pursue excellence in all our activities. If there's any one attitude I want to see at Hewlett-Packard, it's a healthy dissatisfaction with the status quo. Total quality control provides a discipline for translating that into real results. It's a way of institutionalizing a continuous process of organizational self-renewal.

IBM

Corporate Background

IBM began in 1911 in Endicott, New York. It was formed when the International Time Recording Company, the Computing Scale Company, and the Tabulating Company merged and incorporated in New York State as the Computing-Tabulating-Recording Company (C-T-R). It manufactured commercial scale, tabulating, and time recording equipment. In 1914, at the age of 40, Thomas J. Watson became its president. By the end of 1940 C-T-R had 1,346 employees, manufacturing plants in Endicott, Dayton, and Washington DC. Its gross income was $4 million. In 1924, C-R-T adopted the name of IBM.

IBM's operations are primarily in the field of information-handling systems, equipment, and service to solve the increasingly complex problems of business, government, science, space exploration, defense, education, medicine, and many other areas of human activities. IBM products include information processing products and systems, program products, telecommunications systems, office systems, typewriters, copiers, educational and test materials, and related supplies and services. Most products are sold or leased through IBM World Wide Marketing Organization. Selected products are marketed and distributed through authorized dealers and remarketers.

IBM is truly an international buyer, developer, manufacturer, and seller with development laboratories, manufacturing sites, and sales and service offices located throughout the free world. To support these activities, IBM employs more than 400,000 people. Due to the highly technical nature of our business and the rapid growth of the techology, IBM invests heavily in research, development, and engineering. For example, in 1986 a total of $5.2 billion was invested representing 10.2 percent of our growth income. IBM worldwide growth income in 1986 was $51.25 billion.

Interview with John F. Akers
Chairman of the Board

Do you have an official quality policy?

Product leadership through quality is one of our corporate goals. Our objective is to offer products and services that are defect-free. To accomplish this, we know that each stage of the process that produces those products and services must be defect-free. We believe that if each individual strives for and achieves defect-free work, we can reach our objective of superior quality both for our customers and for ourselves as a company. This requires that each individual in IBM must assume a personal responsibility for performing defect-free work.

What do you call your quality improvement activities?

Any activity that helps us to better meet our customers' requirements is a quality activity. At IBM we like to think that the next person receiving your work product is your "customer." Any activities that remove defects from the work being transferred at the individual, department, or corporate level are quality activities.

When did you start?

In 1927, the founder and first chairman of IBM, Thomas Watson, Sr., made it clear that our business was built on service to the customer. Since then, each chief executive officer has applied this belief to the needs and challenges of each era. Our recent rededication to excellence started in 1979 with Chairman of the Board Frank T. Cary.

To Mr. Cary, our reputation for quality was only as good as the last machine we shipped or the last customer call we made. He believed that none of us should be satisfied with anything less than 100 percent quality. He believed that we should expect all of our products to be defect-free.

What problems did you have in implementing it?

For one, it's hard to tell people who have been successful that there might be a better way. We started in manufacturing where the management and employees understood the concepts of process and process flow. They were also experienced in ongoing measurements and had results that were highly visible right from the start. As we moved the quality methodologies out of the quality control departments and onto the shop floors, we began to see more improvement. We used these improvements, which were visible and measurable, to convince the development, marketing, and service communities that these techniques really work.

One of the key challenges is to make everyone recognize that senior management is serious about quality. It is senior management commitment that must demonstrate the company is serious in its pursuit of excellence. We believe we hire excellent people and have excellent managers. What senior management did was to provide the environment to permit this excellence to come forward. Some people thought it was a fad and others said, "This too will pass." But the vast majority of people, from the very beginning, have wanted to do a superior job.

This had always been one of our basic beliefs — that every job should be done in a superior way. What we had to do was take the impediments out of the system which were preventing people from doing a superior job. We think we have been successful in doing this in the product area, and we see encouraging results in the nonproduct area. And as I said, we are extending this into our business processes as well.

How did your upper management become involved?

The success of any quality effort is determined by the leadership of the management team. Our executive management team regularly reviews our progress in quality implementation as it impacts products and nonproducts across the corporation. A considerable part of my time is spent defining the strategic direction of the company, of which quality is a key ingredient.

Can you estimate what it cost to implement the process and what savings you realized last year?

We have never been able to put a dollar value on the total cost or the return we have realized from our quality effort companywide. But we have seen in almost every case substantial productivity gains over the long term. Indeed, we believe that quality is a key driver of productivity. Quality focuses on human resource management and job design. Or said another way, people and process. If you couple this with an aggressive capital spending program, which we have been pursuing for the last decade in IBM, you have the ingredients for higher productivity.

We know that by putting more reliable machines in the field, our installation defects have decreased substantially, our repair actions during warranty have decreased substantially, and across the board we can see greater customer satisfaction. All of these translate into a more competitive product. I would not like to think about what our market position would be without these great quality improvements.

For a long time our customers have been differentiating products in the marketplace on the basis of quality. Just to compete, you must have a *high-quality* product. To be an industry leader, you must have a clearly *superior* product. Our users are extremely sophisticated in their application of data processing and information systems. They won't tolerate an inferior product. Thus, our quality savings are really translated into better serving our customer — but then, this is the whole purpose of our company.

What has been the impact on the support areas?

As I said previously, everyone in IBM has a "customer," either internally or externally. Support areas are part of a process that produces products and services. Their support must be defect-free. The quality methodologies have applied as well in the nonproduct area as they have in the product area.

Our methodology encourages the use of ongoing measurement to identify problems rather than to depend on reaction and crisis management. Measurements that are established and documented in our support areas, and particularly in our nonproduct processes, are a simple way of reducing defects. Reduced defects translate into reduced cost and better service.

Do you have a cost of quality system, and if you do, what impact did the improvement process have on reducing the cost of quality?

We have a cost of quality system that is operational in the company. We do not use it as a business measure but more to identify the dollar impact quality has on the business, to identify opportunities for improvement, and to establish a common base for measuring and tracking trends within an organization. Because we are so wide and diverse, a cost of quality comparison across different units of IBM would lose some of its meaning.

In addition, we use special surveys, samples, and site management reviews to gather cost of quality information that may not be visible in our current income and expense statements. These methods taken together permit us to accomplish the objectives stated above and identify opportunities for improvement. Indeed, it does quantify the dollar impact of quality, or the lack of quality, on our business. Because it is within an organization, the focus for improvement activities is highly visible. We do not as a rule correct this at the corporate level. This is done at the business group level and below, where the corrective actions must be applied.

How would you summarize the impact the improvement program has had on your corporation?

We have seen some impressive gains in quality improvement, but we believe our greatest gains are still ahead of us. As the quality movement matures, quality improvement becomes an integral part of the way we do business. The interesting thing is that it feeds on itself. When done correctly, it becomes business as usual.

Our customers have come to expect imaginative designs from the standpoint of reliability, availability, and serviceability. This is an exciting but difficult challenge. It is gratifying that our employees have picked up this challenge and are willing and eager to meet it head-on. Endeavoring to be the best in an ever-growing and complex business is where we find ourselves today.

I have no doubt that our people understand the true meaning of what would happen if we are not the best. It is up to the management of IBM from the corporate office down to the first-line manager to do its part to reinforce the climate of excellence, to use the tools of the quality methodology to focus on process, and to get the defects out. In this way, we all have a job in improving quality.

The underlying common denominator of ongoing quality improvement is that the next task and the next product must have fewer defects and better meet our customers' requirements. I am happy to say that we are achieving this goal.

Motorola, Inc.

Corporate Background

A capital investment of $500 and Paul Galvin's idea to make a battery eliminator launched Motorola's predecessor, Galvin Manufacturing Corp., in 1928. The battery eliminator was a major success because it allowed consumers to operate radios directly from household current instead of from batteries supplied with early models.

In the 1930s the company commercialized car radios under the brand name "Motorola," a new word suggesting sound in motion. As time went on, Motorola also established home and police radio departments, instituted pioneering personnel programs, and began national advertising. Motorola sold its color television receiver business in the mid-1970s and shifted its focus from consumer electronics to high-technology markets in commercial, industrial, and government fields. It is one of the world's leading manufacturers of electronic equipment, systems, and components produced for both national and international markets.

Today Motorola has about 90,000 employees in major facilities in 11 states, 18 countries, and Puerto Rico. It had net sales in 1986 of $5.88 billion with about 30 percent of its business done outside the United States.

Motorola products include two-way and cellular radios, other forms of communications systems, semiconductors, defense and aerospace electronics, automotive and industrial electronic equipment, and data communications and information processing equipment. Motorola communications equipment has been used on most manned and every major unmanned U.S. space mission since Explorer 1 in 1958, including the sophisticated two-way communications gear used in Voyager's grand tour of Jupiter and Saturn, and the radio link that provided voice communication for man's first landing on the moon.

Interview with William J. Weisz
Vice Chairman, Chief Executive Officer

What are the circumstances that led to the company's decision to focus on improvement?

Of course, our whole history and the success that we've had in our various fields has been based on delivering a high quality product at fair value to our customers. We've always strived to do better, but in recent years what has always been acceptable has been challenged as new competition begins to serve the market. So fundamentally I think that the driving force for improvements in quality has come from several directions: first, from our customers where they require an ever-increasing amount of quality and reliability of product as the tasks become more complex; second, from the fact that competition of a quality nature has increased over the last five to 10 years; and third, from the strong desire of our employees to effect improvement through our participative management process.

Were unions involved in any way in the improvement process, and if so, how did they contribute?

We are basically a nonunion company, so the answer is no, unions are not involved in any way in the improvement process. We have always believed we could work better directly with our own people, than with a third party involved. We have built an organization over these almost 60 years of involvement and participation of people at all levels, of consideration for their concerns and their dignity, and to have them as partners in the development of our processes, products, improvements, etc.

Do you have an official quality policy?

Yes we do. For years it was just to deliver quality products. Then in one of our documents, "For Which We Stand," developed in the early 1970s, we made a fundamental statement on the purpose of Motorola. That statement says:

> The purpose of Motorola is to honorably serve the needs of the community by providing products and services of superior quality at a fair price to our customers. To do this so as to earn an adequate profit which is required for the total enterprise to grow, and by so doing, provide the opportunity for our employees and shareholders to achieve their reasonable, personal objectives.

That statement and others in this document really were a formal codifying of what had been the precepts and policies of the company since its beginning. However, as we began to place more emphasis on the improvement of quality, we developed an even more formal statement. It's in our brochure entitled, "Quality Isn't Just Our Motto; It's Our Business." In it we very specifically call out a number of things. First,

Dedication to quality is a way of life to our company and so much so that it goes far beyond rhetorical slogans. Our ongoing program of continued improvement reaches out for change, refinement, and even revolution in our pursuit of quality excellence.

The statement of quality policy says,

It is the objective of Motorola to produce and provide products and services of the highest quality. In all its activity, Motorola will pursue goals aimed at the achievement of quality excellence. These results will be derived from the dedicated efforts of each employee in conjunction with supportive participation from management at all levels of the corporation.

This quality brochure then goes on to discuss the implementation of the policy, and certain other fundamentals. The brochure is published in English, French, German, Japanese, Korean, Malaysian, and Spanish.

What do you call your quality improvement activities?

In 1981, we developed as one of the top 10 goals of the company the *Five Year, Tenfold Improvement Program.* This meant that no matter what operation you were in, no matter what your present level of quality performance was, whether you were a service organization or a manufacturing arm, it was our goal to have you improve that level by an order of magnitude in five years. Today, we carry this forward with a program called *Six Sigma.* *Six Sigma* is a method of design and manufacture that should yield approximately 99.6 percent perfect results. It is the next major step toward 100 percent perfect performance which is the only acceptable goal.

When did this program start?

Well as I said, we have had all sorts of things that impinged upon the quality issue. Our participative management program which has a very high level of quality concern, started in the late 1960s and has been broadened across the corporation since then. The particular increased focus by the policy committee and the development of our initial set of top 10 goals, of which quality was one, started in 1981. Our *Six Sigma* effort started in 1986.

To what sections of the business is it being applied?

It applies across the board. We have been concerned at times that people tended to view quality as applying only to product quality and reliability. Quality and quality improvements apply to everyone, whether it is on the production line, writing up an order, answering the telephone, or dealing with each other in every facet of our corporate life.

What activities were undertaken to start the improvement program?

At a 1981 policy committee meeting we agreed on a very substantial improvement and thus, the five year, tenfold improvement goal. From the setting of the goal at the policy committee level, we fanned out the requirement to have every organization develop goals and action plans to achieve those goals, and milestones by which they could be measured. We incorporated the quality emphasis into every facet of our working environment. It is a key part of our five-year planning procedure. It is a key part of our operational reviews. It is a key part of our communications with our employees. It is a key part of our participative management philosophy. We did use Phil Crosby's books. We distributed a large number of his books around the corporation to managers and many other employees. We created a corporate director of quality, taking one of our most senior line managers who knew the issues with the customer and the problems of the factory design, and had him report directly to our chief executive officer. We have created corporate-wide quality councils and quality councils within each organization. We have had massive training in the corporation. We've used Juran and Deming. We've sent people to Crosby's Quality College. We've used Dorian Shanin's and Stuart Hunter's courses. They are all a part of the effort to train, teach, and increase the dedication to perfection as an absolute in the ongoing culture of Motorola.

What problems did you have in implementing this program?

The first issue that had to be addressed was the attitude of some that we had been delivering good enough quality to satisfy the customer. The second issue was that quality was a trade-off against cost; that is, if you wanted better quality, you had to pay more for it in the cost of the product. We had to address those two issues.

It takes a lot of effort and a lot of work, but we convinced people that quality is a matter of survival and that there's a lot of excellent competition out there. Secondly, we made great use of Crosby's book, *Quality Is Free*, as a means of showing people that quality truly is free. While it does require an initial investment, it pays back very quickly if you do perfect quality work. Today that story is understood and, more importantly, committed to across the company.

Once we had those issues addressed, we had to train our people in all the things that would allow them to deliver better quality. That ranged all the way from courses in statistical control, courses available from our Motorola training unit, and specialized courses for engineers, to a myriad of additional things we did to increase the culture and improve the training and get the commitment.

How did you get your upper management involved with this activity?

The upper management was really there from the beginning because the policy committee is composed of the top 12 managers in the corporation, line, and staff. They developed the goal and subscribed to it whole-heartedly. On a monthly basis the operating committee of the corporation, comprised of many of the same managers, measures the progress of each of the line and staff organizations. And on a regular basis throughout the year, each key manager had to report on his progress toward achieving the milestones in the five year, tenfold improvement program. We also recognize achievement of various kinds throughout our sectors and groups. An example is the Chief Executive Office Quality Award, which is presented by one of us in the chief executive office, whenever appropriate, to any individual or organization for a uniquely superior contribution to improved quality and reliability. Each of our major businesses has quality councils, where the senior managers from all disciplines meet and discuss progress. These councils are, in effect, the steering activity for all subordinate programs.

Can you estimate what it costs to implement the process and what savings you realized?

No, I really can't say what it costs to implement the process. In hard dollars I don't think it is very much. The amount of time invested for everyone to become involved is significant. But it is an absolutely required investment. As far as the net cost, I think we can demonstrate in many ways that we are reducing our net costs substantially and saving time as a result of doing all the things that we are doing, rather than having it increase the cost or take more time.

What has been the impact on the support areas? By support areas, we're talking about the product operation function, or manufacturing function, which is traditionally where people focus.

Well, I think it has been very positive. First of all, I think it has always been true that people want to do a quality job. And given the opportunity and the support to do that job, they will perform in that fashion. After all, they are consumers too, and they want to deliver product to their customers as they wish it to be delivered to them. Because we have made our emphasis on quality across the board, we have the ability to involve people, to get them excited, to get them to be supportive and to measure them in all activities, whether they be purchasing or personnel or corporate management information systems, etc.

Do you in fact have a cost of quality system, and if you do, what impact did the improvement process have on reducing cost or improving quality?

Yes, we do have a cost of quality system. Really it should be called the cost of *poor* quality. We have it incorporated in all sectors of the company, including the corporate level. The system is being used to a very good degree in many places, and it's just being learned in others. We are forecasting improvements on a continuing basis, and we're using it as a major benchmark of our success because we don't believe there is any success or quality improvement unless there is an associated reduction in cost.

Can we discuss some specific examples of improved performance?

Here are just a few of what we believe are significant breakthroughs:

Our Mobile Products Division (Communications Sector) has a manufacturing operation in Mount Pleasant, Iowa, that produces a line of economy priced two-way mobile radios for use in vehicles. One of the key customer satisfaction measurements used by the operation was on-time delivery of this product per the committed customer schedule dates for orders. This measurement was 99.8 percent in 1979 which was considered excellent at that time.

In mid-1979, a major quality improvement effort was mounted across Motorola, and the Mount Pleasant facility considered areas that it could improve. The plant management reviewed improving the delivery performance, and the question most asked was "why?" After considerable discussion and study, it was decided that striving for excellence in delivery and a 100 percent record was worth the additional efforts. The management structured improvement teams around the functional areas involved in delivery performance, such as purchasing, manufacturing, production, order administration, etc., and studied the problem and developed action plans to impact the problem areas. New procedures and disciplines were implemented which at first seemed burdensome, but after a time became routine. The entire operation became united in a singular object of perfect delivery. In early 1980 the plant achieved its first month of 100 percent delivery to the ship schedules committed to the customers. The next month was again perfect delivery, and the next, and the next. As the milestones were reached for six months, one year, two years, etc., of perfect delivery, the pride of accomplishment became infectious. The attitude of plant personnel, component suppliers, interplant support groups, and others changed such that during times of part shortages, short delivery orders, and order paperwork problems, the attitude was not the old accepted norm of "whose problem is it" but to the participating "what can I do to help?"

The Mount Pleasant, Iowa, operation has now achieved more than eight years of continuous 100 percent delivery to schedule month after month. More than 255,000 orders have been shipped without a *single* miss of scheduled dates. Perfection has been achieved.

In our Automotive and Industrial Electronics Group, the wave soldering defects rate at our Stotfold, United Kingdom plant was reduced 250 times as part of a two-year program there. Where reject rates were once more than

5,000 parts per million, they now run under 20 parts per million. A lot of planned experiments were first conducted to determine those parameters most critical for solder joint quality. Within six months the defect rate of printed circuit (PC) boards had been reduced to approximately 1,500 parts per million by optimizing the solder line speed, the angle of the board entry into the wave, and the preheating of the line to the optimum temperature.

Further progress in quality improvements was realized through the use of new soldering flux and the redesign of PC boards. The latter change included use of diamond pads, relocation of chip components, and other geometrical changes to minimize solder shorts.

This example typifies many similar improvements in soldering defects that have been achieved across the corporation.

The Communications Sector is involved in the design, manufacture, installation, and service of communications equipment. In the early 1970s, efforts at improving product reliability were focused on component qualifications and evaluation of equipment operation over environmental extremes such as temperature and vibration. With the continuing need for higher reliability from the market, these methods were proving inadequate.

The Reliability Engineering Group in the Portable Products Division of the Sector in Fort Lauderdale, Florida, began experimentation in 1975 to develop a sequential Environmental Stress Test Program for its products that could be correlated to actual field failure rates. The group evaluated different techniques such as temperature extremes, thermal shock/cycle, dust, humidity, mechanical shock, power life testing, and other stresses, until a test matrix was obtained that correlated to the failure rates that had been measured in actual customer applications. The end result was an eight-week Accelerated Life Test (ALT) that precipitated the correct failure modes and, with an acceleration factor, could satisfactorily predict the product field failure rate over a five-year use period. In 1978 the division began to use this ALT evaluation on new radio designs prior to shipment to measure their reliability and correct design deficiencies.

The Communications Sector management concluded that the ALT methodology was a valuable reliability tool for use in all new products and required that each of the many equipment divisions of the Sector develop and correlate an ALT for its product families. Today, these ALTs are documented in standard operating procedures and are performed at prototype and pilot run stages on all major new product development programs. Reliability goals are set at the start of development of each product, and the ALT must demonstrate that the product has achieved its goal prior to introduction. The ALT has played a major role in the Sector, improving its product reliability by a factor of approximately 10 times over a five-year period.

The Discrete Group of our Semiconductor Products Sector has seen a dramatic improvement in product quality levels. In a period of 1974 through 1979, the average outgoing quality improved 72 percent, or three-fold. During the five years, 1980 through 1986 (covering a period of our *Five Year, Tenfold Improvement Program*), the average outgoing quality improved greater than tenfold, with electrical and visual/mechanical AOQ ending the year at less than 100 parts per million. Many, many factors of our overall quality program, including state-of-the-art advancements, contributed to this significant success. And it is this success, I believe, that has made us a quality leader in the discrete semiconductor business worldwide.

How would you summarize the impact the improvement program has had on your corporation?

Monumental. First of all, when we set the original five-year, tenfold goal, we weren't too scientific about it. We argued for a long time about how much it ought to be per year, what it ought to be, would it be too much, too little. We finally concluded that we really had to make it substantive, had to make it very "reach out," and we picked an order of magnitude in five years, as a very reach-out goal. At the time we did it, I don't believe there were very many people in our policy committee who thought we were going to achieve it. Yet we found, generally speaking, that in most places around the corporation we exceeded the milestones.

Our experience to date underscores again the precept that if you set high expectations and give people the support and opportunity they need, they can achieve. However, we still have a way to go to achieve all of our goals. We have some places that are doing superbly and some places that are not. So there is still a lot yet to do for us to be feeling even relatively comfortable.

Is the rate of improvement still accelerating at Motorola?

Yes, I think it is. I think it is because people are seeing the results of significant effort. In fact, the most difficult time was in the early phases, when people were spending a lot of time, effort, and investment and had not begun to see it in the results in the factories and in the field. There was a lot of frustration and concern by managers that with all this effort going on, they really were not yet being able to measure definitive results. Then we crossed that hurdle — went past the level of having it flow through — and began to definitively measure substantive improvements. It's like a snowball. As people began to see the improvements, first little bits and then dramatic, they got even more excited about what they were doing. The enthusiasm is higher today than it was at the beginning. And the opportunity is just as great for continued improvement.

So it sort of reinforces itself?

It reinforces itself continuously.

Can you comment further on how you arrived at the original goal of tenfold improvement for a five-year planning period?

Well, frankly there isn't much additional to say. We literally decided on it, as I indicated, to make it difficult to achieve, yet make it something that was easily understood and could be used as a rallying cry across the corporation. So rather than being a complicated formula different for each organization, five years, tenfold is simple, is understood by everybody, and everybody can start from his own absolute point of performance and measure his improvement.

Can you outline the company's future quality improvement plans and goals?

Because of our success in the *Five Year, Tenfold Improvement Program,* all of our people are very excited and enthusiastic. The new goals in our *Six Sigma* program are based on our past experience and our belief that through "reach out," they are attainable. We're certainly increasing the pace of our training in a whole host of areas. Our participative management programs are generating more ideas, more concerns, more improvements. We are going to do benchmarking in greater detail than we have ever done before in measuring every phase of our performance against two factors: these are, first, our competition, whoever that may be, in whatever field, in whatever process, and in whatever function, and second, against the ultimate in terms of service to the customer. Our *Six Sigma* improvement program is the flagship of Motorola's never-ending improvement process.

3M

Corporate Background

3M was founded in 1902 in Two Harbors, Minnesota, on the shore of Lake Superior. Originally conceived as a mining company, 3M floundered for a number of years. In 1916, however, things began to change. The company established its first formal testing laboratory, and paid a dividend of 6¢ per share.

In the early 1920s, 3M developed its first innovative product — waterproof sandpaper. Another milestone occurred in 1925 when a young laboratory assistant invented masking tape. Masking tape represented 3M's first step toward diversification and was the first of the family of Scotch brand pressure-sensitive tape.

3M's emphasis on research and development led to expertise in such technologies as precision coating and bonding, fluorochemistry, nonwoven fabrics, and imaging and electronics. Today, the company markets about 50,000 products in such diverse markets as health care, electronics, graphic arts, and adhesives and abrasives.

The company is organized into over 50 divisions and departments, and is well known for spawning innovative products in these relatively small business units. The line business units are grouped into four sectors: Electronic and Information Technologies, Graphic Technologies, Life Sciences, and Industrial and Consumer.

3M sales in 1984 totaled nearly $8 billion, and the company employs about 87,000 people worldwide. 3M has operations in 53 principal locations outside the United States, with manufacturing facilities located in 31 countries.

Interview with Allen Jacobson
Chairman of the Board and Chief Executive Officer

Do you have an official quality policy?

A quality statement was developed to communicate the commitment and direction of our quality emphasis to both employees and external publics: "3M will develop, produce, and deliver, on time, products and services that conform to customers' expectations." The policy also spells out specifically what is meant by "conformance to expectations," that is, "these products and services must be useful, safe, reliable, environmentally acceptable, and represented truthfully in advertising, packaging, and sales promotions." An implementation statement accompanies the policy to affirm that we will manage our business to ensure that "conformance to expectations" is the goal of the entire company. This statement also identifies specific objectives: 3M will measure the cost of quality in all departments, divisions, groups, business sectors, and international subsidiaries; 3M will ensure conformance to personal, product, service, and regulatory requirements on a worldwide basis; and, 3M will communicate its commitment to quality to its customers through policy and performance.

What do you call your quality improvement activities?

We refer to quality improvement activities in a number of ways: quality emphasis, quality process, and quality evolution. None of these terms connotes a finite program, nor are the activities limited to specific sections of the organization. We believe that quality improvement must be approached as a universal, infinite evolutionary process.

When did it start?

We have always placed quality as a high priority in our business, but our new thrust on quality started in 1979 and is continuing today because it has become part of our management system.

To what sections of the business is it applied?

Our improvement process is directed at all parts of our business. It penetrates every corner. That is the way to get the most out of the activity. Directing it at manufacturing alone is just poor business.

What activities were undertaken to start the improvement process?

3M's strategy is focused on two interrelated factors: the recognition that organizational quality affects product and service quality, and that a well-defined quality policy and objectives are needed to guide all of management through functional processes. Five key concepts of quality are the primary quality philosophies that define 3M's approach.

The first of these states that quality is defined as "consistent conformance to customer expectations," not as a value-oriented, elusive "goodness" that products just "have." The objective is to relate quality directly and specifically to a product's fitness for use. That is, what the external customer requires of a product to achieve satisfaction, and what the internal requirements are to meet that customer's requirement. Vital to this process is how well each separate function within the organization understands its role and requirements. Once the external customer expectations have been translated internally, the word "customer" applies to the next person or area to receive someone else's work, and that work then becomes a "product." In this way, each person and function within 3M can affect quality, no matter how far removed they are from the finished product that is delivered to the external customer.

The second key concept is "prevention." To achieve conformance to expectations is to prevent errors from occurring, rather than to try detecting and sorting through them. We use specific improvement projects to accomplish this.

The third key concept is the measurement of quality through indicators of customer satisfaction. Identifying customer satisfaction indices creates measurements that focus improvement on areas that will yield the greatest return, and identifies the degree to which we are satisfying customer expectations.

The fourth concept, and ultimate goal of any quality improvement effort, is 100 percent conformance — absolutely no errors or failures. And, although a performance standard of 100 percent conformance may never be attained, as a goal it is a commitment to continuing quality improvement and conformance to expectations.

The last concept is commitment — commitment that starts at the top and recognizes that quality improvement does not just happen. Quality improvement has to be planned and actively managed if it is to become a way of life. The critical challenge is to create individual, personal commitments throughout the organization.

In 1979, 3M began to develop its approach to quality, based on the five concepts. The result is a corporate quality emphasis that works well with our decentralized structure, focusing on individual divisions, staff groups, and subsidiaries. Each business unit is responsible for developing and implementing its own quality effort within broad corporate guidelines. This approach recognizes the traditional autonomy of 3M's line businesses and accommodates the wide variety of customers and products that need to be handled by individualized quality improvement processes. As each business unit is introduced to quality improvement, the corporation stresses three tasks for success.

The first of these tasks is the development of a strategy and process for quality improvement to create the necessary changes in employee attitude and organization — not as a short-term program, but as a way of life. The second task is analysis of all systems and functions, and documentation through an objective audit of the unit's approach to quality. The third is an expressed commitment to implementing deliberate changes in products and services. The ultimate objective is for each business unit to develop a consistent process that will ensure product quality. This is extremely important to a company like 3M which expects 25 percent of its annual sales to come from products developed within the previous five years. In today's competitive environment, it is critical that new product introductions be done right the first time, or costs and marketing mistakes will quickly turn a potentially successful new product into a failure.

The overall corporate quality emphasis is guided through a corporate quality improvement team. The team is comprised of 3M's senior management: the chief executive officer, the executive vice presidents of our business sectors, the vice president of finance, and our two senior staff vice presidents. Together, they set corporate quality policy and define overall business objectives. In addition, they work closely in their individual organizations to integrate quality costs and other standards into their reporting systems.

How was the quality emphasis implemented?

The quality emphasis is introduced to each business unit using the annual improvement plan which is part of the unit's operational and strategic business plan. Each unit develops its own strategy and action plan to meet the specific needs of its businesses and customers. Usually there are four phases. First, management works through a planning stage to gain an understanding and awareness of quality. Second, management forms a quality improvement team within the business unit. Often the team leader reports directly to the general manager, and is assigned full-time responsibility for quality implementation. The team is made up of representatives from each major function within the business unit, and includes key staff people. The team is charged with the responsibility for developing a specific action plan for quality improvement. The third phase is the creation of on-site quality improvement teams. These include all areas of operations, such as plants, sales branches, laboratories, and warehouses. The fourth phase is error identification and measurement, where actual quality improvement begins.

It's been our experience that nonproduction areas have had the most difficult time setting priorities for error identification and the development of effective measurement indices. However, by doing a functional analysis first, any staff or line unit should be able to develop an effective process.

The ongoing quality process requires many other concepts and approaches, including project teams, improved systems, problem solving, SPC, and others.

What problems did you have in implementing it?

We had some minor problems but no more resistance than to other changes. In fact, I believe it was well-accepted by most of our employees and the management team.

How did your upper management teams become involved?

In 1979, top management under Lew Lehr, then 3M's chief executive officer, believed that the improvement process should be adapted by 3M. As a result, our corporate staff quality department was formed in 1980.

What has been the dollar impact of the quality emphasis?

Even after five years, it's not easy to specify how all our quality improvement activities translate into profit and loss figures. We've had a good deal of experience in tallying manufacturing savings, but, when it comes to some of the other areas, it's still hard to get an exact reading.

But the impact is there, and it's becoming dramatic. It's safe to say that in the last five years we have saved close to a quarter of a billion dollars in quality costs.

North American Tool and Die Company

Corporate Background

In 1978 North American Tool and Die was a marginally profitable small manufacturer with an unenthusiastic work force. Today its sales have more than quadrupled — profits are more than seven times what they were and employees believe it is a great place to work. Turnover has fallen from 27 percent to four percent; absenteeism is one percent. Thomas H. Melohn, President and Chief Executive Officer of NATD, says that he is on a crusade to change the "coloration of American executives" and to accomplish three goals: (1) expand the company and raise profits, (2) share with employees whatever wealth is created, and (3) have fun.

Productivity and profits have improved since 1978, as well as the quality of work life for employees. The customer reject rate of products has declined from five percent to one tenth of one percent. NATD has been named "Vendor of the Year" eight times in the last four years by four companies and is the preferred vendor for such corporations as Digital Equipment Corporation, Dataproducts, Hewlett-Packard, and Apple.

NATD's noteworthy approach to manufacturing has resulted in no less than a dozen articles in local and national press. In 1984 *Savvy* magazine named NATD as one of nine U.S. companies offering women the best opportunities. A PBS television documentary on *In Search of Excellence* by Peters and Waterman featured NATD. In January 1987, *Inc.* magazine published an article on how NATD hires great employees.

Perhaps Melohn's working wardrobe of loud golf pants, golf shirts, and blue blazers is responsible for his company's complete turnaround within a decade. But more likely, the cause is the unorthodox executive's dedication to improving the quality of product and quality of work life for employees.

Interview with Tom Melohn
President, North American Tool and Die Company

You were in marketing with a big corporation for 25 years. Why did you change jobs and become president of North American Tool and Die?

I got sick and tired of the corporate politics, inertia, back-stabbing, buck-passing, and lack of prudent risk-taking to the point I had to get out. I had all the trappings of success as a senior vice president of a half-billion-dollar company, but personally and professionally I was very unhappy. I decided that at age 47 I didn't want to spend the next 18 years "leading a life of quiet desperation," so I just had to get out. It wasn't worth it.

Why did I go to North American Tool and Die? Several reasons. We wanted to stay in the San Francisco Bay Area because of the quality of life. It didn't take a genius to see that Silicon Valley was a high growth area, but we didn't have the money to buy a computer company. Nor did we have the guts to go into the computer business per se, because we found that we would be dependent on someone else's R&D expertise. We'd start out giving him 10 percent of the stock, then 25, and then 50, and then he'd leave to start his own company. It's kind of like buying a French restaurant — the chef's got you. We then looked at other industries that served high technology and we figured that if we got with ancillary industries that rode with the product class that was growing at 30 percent a year, we'd enjoy it, without the capital expenditures and the dependency on one genius.

So, we happened upon the job shop industry. I didn't even know what a job shop was! But what we saw was a cottage industry. There are 3,000 job shops in the Bay Area alone, and we saw a product class that had an enormous strategic gap. It didn't take a genius in 1977 to see that the Japanese were coming and that American job shops were providing 10 to 15 percent rejects.

So we went to about 50 buyers and 25 engineers — we didn't know any of them — to try to get a profile. We asked, "What are you looking for in a job shop?" And they said, "Quality, service, price, quality, service, price." Coming out of the food industry I didn't believe that, because there, at a quarter of a cent per pound, you either got the order or you didn't, quick. We tested that pretty hard. What they were saying is, "Hey, look. Give me parity pricing, but if you can give me a part that's to print, and if you can get me a part to print on time, there's an enormous void." So that gave us our strategy.

So we took the top 10 job shops in the Bay Area and went down the list looking for ones for sale, with the objective of finding a company that had the capability of providing the two customer needs of quality and service, in that order.

I took out a second mortgage on my house to buy a job shop. When I told my wife what we were going to buy, she panicked, because — and I'm not kidding — I can't put the license plate on my car, and I can't read a blueprint. She asked, "How are you going to contribute to that business?" And I said, "We're going to change the name to 'Midlife Crisis Industries.'"

Do you have an official quality policy?

For a while, when we first came here, some people were very nervous, and they asked, "What are your policies?" And we said "We don't have any, except for these things: be honest, be fair, treat other people the way you want to be treated, and one tenth of one percent reject, maximum one tenth of one percent reject, maximum one tenth of one percent reject." The whole reason for our being is one tenth of one percent customer rejects, period. That's it.

Is better equipment the answer to improved quality?

If it is, we're in deep trouble. You saw the equipment out there. Except for a couple of pieces, it looks like Civil War stuff. The tool room didn't even have a jig bore. Our philosophy here, and it is etched in stone, is that you can have $100,000 capital assets, $1 million, $10 million, $100 million, $1 billion, but you don't have a thing unless you have good people who care to run those assets. Period. State-of-the-art laser? Forget it. If you don't have good people that care to run those machines, you haven't got a thing. So no, sir, better equipment is not the answer. That does not mean you take jobs that you are not equipped physically to do. That doesn't mean that at all; but state-of-the-art equipment doesn't get you better quality. Period.

What is your approach to people managememt?

Oh, boy. Real easy. It all starts with one immutable fact: Those folks out there on the plant floor are absolutely no different than you and I. You treat people the way you want to be treated. I had one gal call from a major national business magazine and say, "Well, gee, what you're doing out there, that's indigenous to Silicon Valley with beer-busts and parties and sandals and all that stuff." We're not Silicon Valley! This is Hamtrammack; this is Newark; this is Hammond; this is Gary; this is hot, dirty, noisy, dangerous, and mass production. No white rooms here; no clean rooms here. This is the heart of America in microcosm out there; it really is. You treat people just the way you want to be treated.

Would you expand on your principles related to delegating?

I can't read a blueprint; I can't go out and set up a die or make a die or a fixture. So we hire good people that are professionals, that care. They define the problem, and I get out of their way and let 'em go solve it. And that also, by the way, helps them to grow enormously. It's a neat way to manage, because they never come in here with a technical problem — never — because they know I can't do anything about it. They have to solve it out there, and that's where it should be solved.

It seems like the morale of the people is so high, so uniquely high. What have you done?

They're neat people. Incredible human beings. What it really gets down to is caring about them. You've got to care about those people. They're the ones who are getting one tenth of one percent reject; I'm not.

Let me make an analogy. When's the last time you got a compliment from your boss? A real compliment? Not, "Good job, Jim." But a real compliment. My God, think about that. Why don't they give compliments any more? If you get good people and they're doing a good job, you compliment them. Sincerely. You recognize their achievements because they're the ones who are really doing it. You recognize it personally: "Hey, Joe, that's a super job you did, and I really mean it." You recognize them publicly in front of their peers, and you recognize them in their paycheck. *And* you do it quickly, you don't do it eight years after they accomplish something. Is that any different than the way you want to be treated?

Then you build the family feeling. The people help each other. You communicate with them, and let 'em know what's going on. Every month we get everybody together on the day and night shift and tell them exactly what's going on. Backlogs, sales, new orders, old orders, everything. Everything. Because it is their company, and they have a right to know. I don't want any rumors; I don't want any rumors at all. So you tell it absolutely bone straight. Because that's the way you want it, isn't it? And they're no different. You try to care about them. And guess what — then they'll care about you too.

What do you do to ensure that you're hiring good people?

We look for people who care: they care about themselves, their family, their company, their future. How do you tell those things? I couldn't care less how they look physically. I don't care if they have beards or long hair, as long as it's neat. If you look at the physical appearance of a person, it's kind of like a phrenological peek into their being. If they dress sloppy and are dirty, then they're probably going to be that way. I don't mind long hair; I don't mind unique clothes, as long as they are clean and neat. And I look for people who believe in the work ethic. I also look at the job applications; that's another window into the soul. If those applications are messy and sloppy, the people will probably be the same way. I don't mean poor grammar, but is it neat? I don't care about spelling. I don't care that they can't write English well. But is it neat and filled out completely? Did you ever look at the Other

Interests section? "None." Hobbies? "None." What does that tell you? What usually is a good indicator are the extracurricular activities — church, Little League, soccer coach. . .These are the signs of a person who wants to be part of his or her community, that the person wants to give of himself and be part of something larger.

Then you listen during the interviews. Listen to their questions. They can tell a lot. You see, an interview's a two-way street. They get to interview us just as much as we interview them. I'll give you two instances.

Here's Applicant A's questions: "What are the paid holidays? What's the vacation? What's the medical insurance?" What does that tell you? Now contrast that to Applicant B: "What do you make here? How long have you been in business? Who are your customers?" I don't mean they have to be *Harvard Business Review* questions, but do you see the difference? That's who you look for.

I don't like people who job-hop. That tells you something else. Now that's a little dangerous, with the layoffs that have gone on in this area during the past couple of years. But if you see somebody that's one year here, two years there, one year, one year — be careful. You look for people who want tenure, because we don't want turnover. I don't mean just the dollar cost, but the cohesiveness of the family. We don't want turnover. Our turnover here is less than four percent a year. Silicon Valley? It's running about 30 percent a year. And I don't want turnover because we lose the cohesiveness of the family. I want good people and I want them to stay.

It seems like honesty was the key ingredient in your improvement. How has this paid off for you?

Let me give you an example from back in my own corporate first life. Here's your annual job evaluation. Above average, average, average, above average, above average, average — and then you're terminated. Now, this is how it *should* be done: "You're doing a super job in these areas. But in these areas, you need to improve. And here is how *we* are going to work it out." When you don't tell people that and you get into this "average, above average syndrome," and they're 54 years old, and they're canned, number one, that ain't honest; number two, that ain't smart; number three, that ain't fair to the employee; and number four, that ain't fair to the company. So you've got to be honest, absolutely bone honest.

I'll give you an example of how this pays off. We made a die for a customer, and we quoted $20,000. We overran the cost on that die by $16,000. Typically, the first thing you do is go back to the customer and whine and cry: "I missed this, and I missed that, and you didn't tell me this." We don't do that. You see, a deal is a deal — with your employees and with your customer. We said that we would make that die to print for $20,000. Now it's up to us to do that. If we miss, that's our nickel.

Now what happens with most other companies? They start crying, right? We don't do that, and our toolmakers know that. They know exactly how many hours are in that die, they know the shop rate, they know the dollars, and they saw that I wasn't going back. I told them I wasn't going back to the customer. We made a deal. We gave our word.

Now what do you think our toolmakers came away with? The guy's straight. Can I quantify that? No. That's what you call trust. I am absolutely convinced that one of the reasons for our success is that we are absolutely straight with our customers, absolutely straight. If we say we're going to make the part and deliver it on time, it'll be on time. We have never shipped a first article late in seven years, except once. We were seven days late. When we called the buyer, he just laughed.

That's a refreshing attitude.

Well, the tragedy is that you say it's refreshing. That's the real tragedy. And tragically, it *is* refreshing. But see, our employees see that, and they know we're straight, and then we have trust.

Not only that, but after this period of time, they have probably come to accept that a commitment on the part of management is a commitment to them.

It isn't a commitment on the part of management. It's a commitment on the part of all of us. I'm not president; I'm head sweeper. We're all in it together. There's a big difference, because when I start saying I'm management and they're labor, we're in trouble, even in here. Then you start getting a big office, and you start getting a Mercedes, and the preferred parking places, and working half days, and dipping into the till, and all the other games. I don't want that. It's not fair. It's not right. And it doesn't work. The "I've got mine, now you get yours syndrome" doesn't work. That's why American business is in deep trouble.

Let me show you something. This is a cartoon of a guy sitting in a big plush office, right? Behind the big desk, the plush chair, and the employee's standing there, and the boss says, "Come in, Frank, I've been eager to communicate downward to you." You got it? No way. No way.

How do you recognize your employees for doing a good job?

Same way you want to be recognized. You want to have praise, you want it from "the boss," you want it in front of your peers, from your peers, in your paycheck, and quick. I wander around the plant, and the old owner — God love him, he was and is an incredible person — used to tell me, "Go out in the plant and snoop." I don't want to go out in the plant and snoop. They're good people. They're professionals. What am I snooping for? If I feel I have to snoop, I hired the wrong people. But what I do is go out in the plant and wander around two or three times a week and ask, "How are you doing?" And some of them still say, "I'm working on the countersink." "That isn't what I asked you. *How* are you doing? Not *what* are you doing? *How* are you doing?" "Oh, great." "Got any problems?" "Yeah, this countersink is sticking." "Have you talked to your lead man; have you talked to your foreman? I'll leave a note on the plant manager's desk." But I'm not out there finding out *what* they're doing; I'm finding out *how* they're doing. And they know. They know that I'm interested, that I care.

You do a lot of on-the-spot recognition. Can you give me an example of a couple of instances where you recognized people immediately?

Yeah. I wandered around and asked our machine shop foreman what he was doing. He said, "I'm working on X job. I hope to automate it." And I said, "Let me know when it's done; I'd love to see it." He came in a week ago Monday and said, "Okay, it's running." So I went out and looked, and I flipped. Now before I did anything, I got the head engineer, the plant manager, and quality control. Had they signed off on it? There's no sense praising somebody if it doesn't do the job. Make sure it's blessed. And once they bless it, then I get out there. He was leaving for Germany on Sunday, so I said good-bye to him on Thursday, gave him a check, and told him to have some fun in Europe. He knew how I felt — as a human being and as a boss. And I rewarded him in the pocketbook, and quick. Don't give him an award eight years later. That's stupid.

Some people ask, "What are you giving him a check for? That's part of his job." But he's going the extra mile. He thought of that thing driving home. He worked on it after hours, after shift. He didn't even punch in again. Now he wins twice, three times. Personal recognition and the paycheck, plus the profitability of that job will take our gross margin up more, which will increase our pre-tax, which will increase the value of his stock. We all win. And see, all his fellow employees know that in varying degrees.

You have "super-people meetings." Can you explain that program?

Sure. First of all, "super person" is limited only to machine operators. It never includes department heads, lead men, foremen. It's the machine operators. It's the ones who really get it done. Number two, it can be any employee, and it can be the same employee 48 months in a row. We have our super-person-of-the-month meeting between the 10th and the 20th of the month following the month that we're recognizing. And we get the day and the nightshifts together (it's on overtime, and obviously we pay overtime automatically), so we have a reinforcement of the family — the cohesiveness. And then we play charades. I'll say the super person this month is a man. And they'll start guessing. Three-time winner. They'll start guessing. Day shift.

Machine shop. And they'll start guessing. And then they guess it's Joe. We'll all whoop and holler, and Joe comes up and I give him a check for $50. Big deal, huh? But more important, the name goes on that plaque, and that *is* a big deal. What we're really doing is recognizing their self-worth.

It's never an award based on yield. It's always for greater efficiency, quality. Something smarter, something better.

How do you train your employees?

Well, obviously, *I* don't. The foremen do, and the lead men do. I really don't know how they do it, and don't want to know. What I do know is they're professionals, and I know they're good, and I know they care, and I know they're training them. Way back, all my friends told me nobody should buy a job shop because all the key men are dying out or retiring. And I said, "Bunk." What does Hewlett-Packard do? What does IBM do? They go to the schools and universities. They spot the early comers and grab them for summer internship. So, I went to the State Department of Education and asked, "Where are the best machine tool technology junior colleges in the state?" One was in Los Angeles, another was Chabot. So I went to the head of the machine tool technology department at Chabot and said, "I want you to come in and tutor our people and I'll pay you." He did, and so we had Chabot University over here every Wednesday night, from 3:45 to 5:00. See, I thought, if you're going to be honest, be honest. Let 'em work on live production. They could scrap it out, but otherwise, it's play. And I wanted it straight; I wanted it real. So they worked on real parts, and it was neat. Anybody could go. I never took grades; I never took attendance. That was between the gang and the professor. The first year's course taught how to be a better machine operator. The second year was how to be a lead man.

You've had some outstanding improvement in the manufacturing areas over the years you've been with this company. Have you seen improvement in other areas besides manufacturing?

There's been an enormous change in quality. An enormous change. After we bought the company, I gave the head of quality control just two rules: one, you report to me, nobody else; and two, don't you dare ship anything unless you bless it. And sometimes he and I got into fights. "I can't see the blemish; come on, will ya? Ship the part." Well, if I cut his legs off, he's done. He's done. Just once. Because he'll remember the one time and so will our fellow employees. He and I have gotten into some good ones; we really have. But you've got to go with him or you're dead.

When you were implementing the family concept, did you run into any problems?

Yeah. The analogy we are talking about classically represents the job shop industry and, I submit, a lot of U.S. manufacturing. They would hire good foremen, but then they'd hire cattle to be the machine operators, give them the minimum wage, kick 'em around, then move them out. We worked for probably nine months to a year, first of all, finding out what kind of business we were in, and second, to start crystallizing some of our management beliefs. These didn't come full-blown, believe me. We tried to retrain, if you will, in a mind-set, and it didn't work very well. We ended up laying off a lot of people at the machine operator level.

Number two in terms of problems was convincing the employees that this was for real. We're talking some pretty idealistic stuff here. Is this for real? When's he going to pull the rug on us? That was a problem we had to deal with. We knew we had to do it straight, honest, every day, every job, every shift, every employee, every problem. And after about two years, they finally realized that it was for real.

I don't like to digress here, but this is fascinating. The correlations with good human beings as fellow employees are awesome. Our absenteeism is less than one percent. Or take industrial accidents — for every $100 of premium, insurance companies pay out $90 in claims. That's average. We pay a $100 premium, they pay out $40 in claims. It's incredible. We get rebates you can't believe. But see, if you get good people that care, the correlations are incredible. Absenteeism, medical, it's incredible. If you put your finger on it, it all comes back to hiring the right kind of human beings.

Now what other problems did we have? It was surprising — well, maybe it wasn't surprising — that selling quality as the strategic point of difference was fairly easy. In retrospect, I guess it was because most people want to do good work.

What impact did the improvement program have on reducing quality costs?

I don't know, because I can't break it down. The impact of the improvements had to reduce the cost of quality because our business has grown 28 percent a year due to the implementation of one tenth of one percent rejects.

Am I right in summarizing that you don't believe it is the "cost" of quality, but the "profit" of quality?

No, I would go more than that. It is the *only* reason for our success. The *only* reason. Why is it that when Silicon Valley generically is in a disaster mode, our toolroom is going 56 hours a week, with an additional third being off-loaded to die shops in the West? Why? Quality.

The quality, customer service, and on-time delivery. The *only* reason.

What advice would you give to the president of a Fortune 500 company?

Remember Marv Thornbury, marvelous Marv Thornbury of the Miracle Mets? Marv wasn't exactly an intellectual heavyweight. "Marv, how'd you do it? How'd you go from 28 games out to winning the pennant in one month?" "I don't know." This went on and on, and he says: "Well, you gotta believe. You just gotta believe." So Mr. CEO, you gotta believe in your people. You've got to believe; that's it. Then let 'em go do their job without second-guessing them. Support them and encourage them. Then when they win, praise them and reward them — and quick.

Is there anything that you believe is important that I didn't direct a question at, that you'd like to mention?

I'll give you an observation. America is in deep, deep trouble. I think we are in a deep recession. I'm not talking Silicon Valley; I'm talking smokestack America. What we are doing is obviously not working. And to hide behind a cocoon of "we can't compete with Japanese, they're subsidized, and they have lower labor costs, and different mores" is a cop-out. What we are doing here at North American Tool and Die isn't *the* way, because there's more than one way to chip up to the green, but it sure is working for us. And if you examine what we've talked about today, you'll find that there isn't one new thing in it. Not one new thing.

Let me leave you with this story. It may be apocryphal, but it sure makes a good point. The late Bear Bryant, coach at Alabama, was in the Sugar Bowl, and Alabama was playing for the national championship. It was the fourth quarter, three minutes left to play, and they were down by five points. Alabama took the kick-off and marched all the way down to the other guys' eight-yard line. Now they had 38 seconds left. The quarterback called time out and went over to the sidelines and said, "Coach, this isn't just for the Sugar Bowl; it's for the national championship. We've got 38 seconds left, and I've got eight yards to cover. What plays do I call?" Bear Bryant took his famous houndstooth cap and tipped it back and said, "Son, you just think for a minute. What plays did you call to get you down here? You go back in there and just keep calling them same plays." And the kid went back in, called the same plays, scored a touchdown, and won the Sugar Bowl and the national championship.

Mr. CEO, in your case those same plays *ain't* workin'. And sure, there's more than one way to chip up a green, but it's working here. I would suggest that you go back to what made this country great and start doing it again. Respect for the individual, teamwork, praise for an honest job well done. End of sermon.

These appendices provide an in-depth insight into the improvement process covered in the body of this book. They include additional interviews with other key executive personnel and specific examples of improvement.

Appendix I – Ford Motor Company

Comments on Quality

by

Harold A. Poling
President, Ford Motor Company

Quality improvement today is receiving a considerable amount of attention from top executives. From your perspective, what is the biggest advantage of quality for your company?

Focusing our efforts on meeting customers' needs and expectations at a price that represents real value to our customers.

What is the most significant change your company has made to improve quality?

Establishing quality as our number one operating priority and redefining quality in customer terms — then showing steady improvement in every aspect of our business.

We often hear about top management commitment to — and line worker involvement in — quality. Convincing the intermediate level that quality is not just a passing fad, however, has been described as "a longer learning process." If the goal is to convince middle management and technical staffs that quality must be a priority equal to cost and schedule, what obstacles remain to achieving that goal?

In the case of Ford, there is no doubt in our organization that quality is our number one priority. Convincing all levels of our organization that this is not a passing fad requires continuous attention, training, and demonstrated action. At Ford, quality is job number one, and our continued demonstration to that commitment will overcome any obstacles that do arise.

What does your company do to measure management performance in the area of quality?

We are committed to continuous improvement in quality. We have an array of in-house indicators and customer feedback mechanisms, and we have developed strong market research programs to keep us abreast of our customers' expectations and how they view our progress. We've redefined quality in terms of the customer's wants and needs. We've recognized that quality and productivity can't be considered as separate business objectives (i.e., improved quality through the elimination of waste enhances productivity).

Once these realities become a part of the "corporate culture," the process of assessing management performance becomes straightforward. This desired change in "culture" requires the commitment of top management to long-term continuous improvement. The assessment of management performance is an effective signal to the organization that top management is serious about that commitment.

In the past, a greater emphasis on quality often meant a bigger quality department. Today, however, the reverse seems to be true in some companies. What changes do you see in the size and organization of your quality function? And what areas will require the most time and attention from your quality department in the future?

You cannot inspect quality into a product and be competitive in today's worldwide competitive environment. Our quality control systems focus on controlling processes to reduce variability and improve product uniformity — a defect *prevention* approach. Our quality systems are being refined to achieve prevention of problems and include much better feedback from our customers regarding product performance in the field over their life cycle.

What advice would you give to a CEO of a major corporation who wants to know the most important thing the CEO can do with regard to quality?

Provide leadership and support leadership in establishing and sustaining quality as the corporation's number one objective, and support through *actions* that cause quality improvement and assure that people have the knowledge, training, and resources to control processes to prevent problems. The objective cannot be accomplished with slogans and no substance.

Would you like to add any other comments about the state of quality in the auto industry, now or in the future?

This is the question I've waited for. With the combined efforts of our people, suppliers, and dealers, we have dramatically improved the quality of Ford cars and trucks in the last four years, and our customers recognize this improvement. But our objective is to build the best quality cars and trucks in the world and have the world know it. This objective is our number one priority and the yardstick by which the marketplace will measure our long-term success.

Ford's Phases in Carrying Out an Operational Philosophy of Continuous Improvement in Quality and Productivity

Awareness

- Recognize the competitive need for improvement in both quality and productivity on a continuous basis.
- Recall that many of our management systems were built on a defect-detection approach, rather than defect prevention; they still function that way, inhibiting improvement in quality and productivity.
- Perceive statistics as a key management tool in making the change to a defect-prevention approach.
- Understand that constructive change requires the active leadership of top company management, mirrored by active participation of the whole company.

Commitment

- Come to a personal understanding of the operating principles for continuous improvement in quality and productivity.
- Adopt a defect-prevention strategy throughout the organization.
- Focus on the control of processes (both technical and administrative), with the involvement of all people, not just specialists.

Preparation

- Identify people skilled in statistics and other disciplines necessary to support the program; hire a consultant if appropriate.
- Establish appropriate training sequences and content for the different levels and functions within the organization — both for job knowledge and for basic statistical understanding; begin statistical training for top and middle management.
- Examine the management systems in effect to identify inhibitors to improvement in quality and productivity; begin to institute necessary change.

Implementation

- Select pilot program sites, where the environment is most favorable for change.
- Provide resources — facilitator/coordinator, training, technical, and financial support.
- Allow time for the pilot programs to show results.
- Expand gradually to other areas, building on the base of experience.
- Extend implementation to suppliers.

Management Support/Institutionalization

- Focus on control of process and problem solving, not on "counting charts."
- Create and maintain a climate for candid two-way reporting of data.
- Establish effective communications with other interdependent activities, to resolve system-related problems.
- Provide continuing involvement, review of results and support.
- Continually reexamine management systems and practices to ensure consistency with operating principles for continuous improvement in quality and productivity.

Appendix II – Avon Products, Inc.

Issue: Purchase Order Development
Print Services Department – New York Office

Performance Indicator

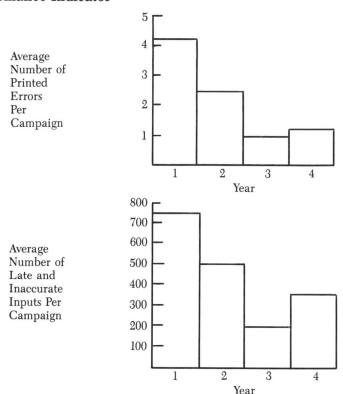

Average Number of Printed Errors Per Campaign

Average Number of Late and Inaccurate Inputs Per Campaign

Background

Printed errors in the purchase order can affect thousands of Representatives every campaign. These errors range from wrong product ordering line numbers and incorrect pricing to incorrect product listings, incorrect unit contents, or misspelled product names. They are the source of hundreds of thousands of PONC dollars as well as dissatisfied Representatives and customers. Most of these errors occur as a result of late, inaccurate, incomplete, or lack of supplier input.

The print services department decided to measure output performance by charting the number of printed errors and late and inaccurate inputs per campaign.

Action Plan

1. Identified input requirements.
2. Developed a master PERT schedule with tie-in to supplier schedules.
3. Initiated performance reporting by suppliers according to agreed on master schedule.
4. Obtained management action to correct supplier lateness.
5. Reorganized purchase order functions to allow responsibility for accounting and to eliminate overlapping functions.
6. Developed and issued a procedure bulletin to clearly establish the "who, what, where, when, and why" of specific input requirements.
7. Established permanent improvement team.

Results

Error-free performance was obtained in the third year for seven consecutive campaigns. The new target is zero defect performance for a full year. Annual PONC reduction is nearly $500,000 through less vendor overtime and increased order processing efficiency at branch locations. A full year of zero defects would result in an operating expense reduction of almost $1 million.

In year four, there is an increase in the incidence of printed errors resulting from a corresponding increase in late and inaccurate input from suppliers. Additionally, there are several new employees who have not completed their orientation programs. These two issues are being addressed by separate improvement teams.

Team Leader

Bill Saunders, Manager, Purchase Order Development

Issue: Excess Brochures
Print Services Department – New York Office

Performance Indicator

Average
Number of Excess
Brochures
Per Campaign

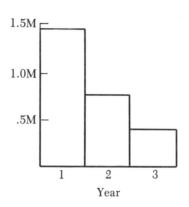

Background

Excess brochures (defined as brochures left unused at the end of a campaign) amounted to 34.3 million books, and cost Avon $3.8 million in 1983 — enough pages to cover Central Park in New York 10 times over! The causes for this excess ranged from inaccuracies in the procedures used in evaluating representative count, their brochure purchase patterns and in projecting for future campaigns; to the method of contracting for brochures from our printing vendors, as well as from inefficiences in our reporting of prescribed free distributions. With the increased emphasis on profitability, it was mandatory that we take steps to reduce this expense.

Action Plan

1. Identified all outlets (users) of our brochures.
2. Verified legitimate outlets, their actual need and reasonable coverage; eliminated unauthorized uses, reduced safety margins.
3. Culled down remaining legitimate outlets to six culprits contributing to excess. Attached a cost of nonconformance to each, with specific action steps to correct.
4. Initiated an education process to change attitudes — from requesting a *cost-free* item to controlling a *costly* item.
5. Defined for management and obtained approval for acceptable operational excess.
6. Analyzed one full year of prior sales patterns to develop and install a trending system to better evaluate Representative's purchase of brochures.

Results

Reduced brochures excess from the average of 1.3 million per campaign in 1983, to .6 thousand in 1984, and even further to .4 thousand year-to-date, 1985 (this is right on plan) — a $2.4 million savings over two years. Established that the only source of planned excess should be for operational needs, which management approved at three percent of sales.

Team Leader

Alvor Brown, Manager, Literature Estimating/Trending

Appendix III — AT&T

Case History in Quality Improvement:
AT&T's Oklahoma City Works
(1983-1985)

The Oklahoma City Works is one of 22 AT&T manufacturing facilities in the United States. Open since May 1960, it has 1.3 million square feet of manufacturing and administrative floor space. The plant's 5,900 employees turn out two flagship product lines, the 5ESS™ switch and the AT&T 3B family of computers. The 5ESS switch is the most advanced digital electronic switching system in the world, and the AT&T 3B computer line ranges in size from a desktop super-microcomputer accommodating from 10 to 25 users to a super-minicomputer that handles up to 100 users.

Between 1983 and 1985, the Oklahoma City Works made major breakthroughs in productivity, quality, and production output. Productivity increased 100 percent in 1984, while cost savings from a sweeping cost effectiveness program mounted to $210 million in that year. From 1983 to 1985, production of the 5ESS switch increased tenfold to 2.5 million lines shipped, and that figure exceeded 6 million in 1985.

A look at more detailed figures shows a similar pattern. For example, engineering changes for the 5ESS switch were reduced significantly between October 1982 and March 1985. Manufacturing intervals were more than halved during this period, while labor efficiency increased dramatically and schedule attainment improved from 30 percent to more than 100 percent.

In January 1985, conducting a rigorous formal acceptance inspection of AT&T 3B20D computers to be used in the management of its telecommunications network, Yoshindo Kanada, director, Inspection Department, Purchased/Products Inspection Division, Nippon Telegraph and Telephone, offered this observation about the Oklahoma City Works: " . . . you are the first American company to pass our inspection the first time . . . you have very good quality."

A study conducted by the United Research Co., Inc., and extensive interviews with plant personnel identified four interrelated factors contributing to this success. Those factors are:

- Management commitment to quality improvement.
- Flagship products that serve as motivators to employees.
- A disciplined business process.
- A good statistical base for pursuing quality improvement.

121

At the same time, a number of quality-related processes, approaches, and tools were used successfully. These included commitment to pursuing quality basics, such as process capability studies and use of process control charts, before attempting to push for a more advanced quality program. Close cooperation with product designers also was a key issue at the Oklahoma City Works, as was training in quality for employees and a quality assurance program for suppliers. The union at the plant was also supportive of the quality improvement program.

Management Commitment

While the United Research Co. study ranked management commitment to the quality improvement program as a key element in its success, additional interviews of employees at the Oklahoma City Works indicated that a few individuals in leadership positions had a marked influence on the outcome of the effort. Those interviewed identified the leadership of the plant's then general manager, A.L. Basey, as significant. Also mentioned as playing important roles were the plant's director of engineering at the time, Larry Seifert, and Robert Hering, the plant's quality control and engineering manager.

Basey believes that effective management is the most important factor in the success of a quality improvement effort. He rates commitment to quality as the most crucial element in such management: "Quality is not part of my job. It is my whole function." According to Basey, commitment is synonymous with action. A manager must do more than sign a memo or letter advocating pursuit of quality — he or she also must be willing to act and make fundamental changes.

At the Oklahoma City Works, for example, more than 70 percent of the equipment and manufacturing processes were installed or updated between 1980 and 1985 to meet the quality requirements of its customers. Also, the culture was transformed to make it more supportive of the pervasive role of quality in the life of the plant.

How was this sweeping change in capital materials, employee attitudes, and values carried off? Basey used a four-part approach to the task.

The first step was to put a good quality management structure in place, beginning with a strong quality manager. Basey's choice was Hering. "I picked Bob not only for his technical knowledge, but also because he knew just about everyone at the plant, which meant he knew who we could count on," Basey said. "Besides that, he has a lot of energy. Basically, you pick the best you have, and you make that person quality czar."

Step two involved convincing other managers — and eventually all employees — that quality is an integral part of their jobs. Frequently, employees try to give that job back to the quality organization, and there is a tendency for the quality organization to take responsibility for it. However, that is not the quality organization's job. It is there to provide a framework and to let people know when they are succeeding or failing in terms of quality. It is also important to convey the message that quality is not a task force job. It is a permanent part of management that has to go on forever. If you ever stop building it, it will fall apart.

To get that and other quality messages across — and it was imperative that they be repeated frequently — Basey used every medium available, from face-to-face meetings with employees to corporate television and the company newsletter.

"This is another example of what I mean by management commitment to quality," Basey said. "I try hard to work quality into every speech I give, into every conversation with employees. That's what it takes to make quality a part of the fabric of an organization.".

Especially notable as a motivator was the Quality Olympics staged to recognize and reward those organizations registering the greatest improvement. Modeled after the International Olympics, then being held in Los Angeles, the opening ceremonies for this campaign included addresses by former Olympic athletes at a gathering of the plant's employees.

In step three, management determined the degree of quality the plant's processes are capable of achieving. This was accomplished by subjecting each one of them to a process capability analysis. "There's no point in trying to achieve a certain level of quality if the plant's processes are incapable of reaching it," Basey explained. "If you don't know what you've got, it's hard to know how to change it."

Finally, in step four, processes were designed to achieve the desired levels of quality. "What really counts is engineering good quality into the processes," Basey said. "When you've done all these things, then you can tell people to give you high quality. When you get the processes right, quality is easy. In fact, it's hard to avoid."

Seifert believes there were three key ingredients in the successful quality improvement effort. The first was building teamwork within the factory, and between units of the factory and outside organizations because no one person can solve quality problems. Teamwork is a practical necessity. On another level, people need goals that go beyond their own organization — what the Japanese call superordinate goals.

Next, it was vital that a clear direction be set, and this is done only by a leader.

Finally, managers had to be willing to do more than set goals and directions. They also found they had to get down in the trenches and help people solve problems. They have to work with them, to go out on the factory floor and find out what is really going on. In Seifert's 18 months at the plant, a thousand different problems were worked out. Some of the problems involved sitting down with people for 15 minutes, finding out what was causing a problem, and, if necessary, blocking and tackling in the organization to help solve the problem. Some of the problems took months to solve.

Flagship Products

A good way to motivate people to strive for quality is to convince them that their work makes a difference. The management of the Oklahoma City Works had an advantage on this score because of the products manufactured at the plant. The 5ESS electronic switch was the first major switching system to be introduced by AT&T since the mid-1970s, and the company obviously had a lot riding on its success.

Meanwhile, some members of the AT&T 3B family of general purpose computers already were performing important tasks in local and long-distance networks, when the entire line was rolled out as the company's initial thrust into the commercial computer market.

The employees of the Oklahoma City Works were accustomed to manufacturing advanced electronic systems. Now they also found themselves in the vanguard of the company's fight for a place in the highly competitive telecommunications and computer markets. And they were proud to be there.

A Disciplined Business Process

In the context of the Oklahoma City Works, the word "discipline" refers to an orderly, prescribed pattern of behavior intended to yield high quality products consistently.

This kind of discipline is pervasive. It is an important part of the initial process capability studies that rigorously pursue one question after another involving a process until no questions remain, and the capabilities of the process and its variables are revealed.

The study team also must be disciplined in defining what it will measure. Team members must follow a formal procedure that results in a common understanding of the things to be measured, and takes into account all the factors bearing on the process.

Finally, discipline is literally engineered into processes so that the people and equipment involved pursue tasks in a well-defined, fully articulated manner that is well understood and fully thought out. For example, some changes in the design of circuit packs require major alterations in the manufacturing process, while others can be accommodated by manually rewiring small portions of the packs. This latter activity is known as "white wiring" and, properly employed, can save significant costs and time. However, unless the people involved in the operation have a clear set of carefully thought out rules as to when to white wire the circuit packs — a function of discipline — the process can result in confusion and costly errors.

Through training and example, discipline eventually becomes a part of every employee's work. "In a factory," Basey said, "you must have this kind of discipline, an orderly discipline. What you're talking about is a cultural change that helps people achieve their full potential."

A Statistical Base

It is given that quality management organizations must have a thorough grounding in statistics to carry out their duties. But if quality is to be everyone's job, then everyone must have some knowledge — albeit rudimentary — of the statistical basis for quality improvement and maintenance. For example, the process control chart that tells operators whether their yield is within acceptable process limits is statistically derived. While operators do not have to be statisticians to use a chart, they can interpret it more easily if they have some understanding of the statistics behind it. And some knowledge of statistics is helpful if the operator is to use the chart to identify opportunities for improving the manufacturing process.

These considerations were behind the ambitious program to train the plant's entire work force in quality basics. Basey supported this effort with his presence at the opening of each training session, which covered such quality basics as process control charts and how to take corrective action when problems are identified.

Begin with Basics

The achievement of excellent quality at the Oklahoma City Works has involved the complex interplay of numerous factors, and has drawn on a broad assortment of tools and procedures, some standard throughout industry, some adapted to the existing situation. Before quality improvement can take place, certain fundamentals must be addressed. At the Oklahoma City Works there were four such fundamentals:

- Process capability studies.
- Process control charts.
- Statistical designed experiments.
- Statistical inspection plans.

Here is a brief examination of each.

Process capability studies. The AT&T Statistical Quality Control Handbook defines a process capability study as "an industrial investigation designed to provide answers to one limited question after another until no further questions are necessary." The studies are crucial for a couple of reasons. First, they highlight the difference between product specifications — what one *wants* to obtain, and process capability, what one presently is *able* to obtain. Besides indicating current process performance, they can lead one to discover what steps must be taken to improve that performance.

The study has several salient characteristics. It should be accomplished through a systems approach — looking not only at the individual pieces of the process, but also at how, or if, those pieces fit together to meet the product's endpoint specification.

The study is usually a team effort involving the product engineer, the operating organization, and the quality engineer. And it is inherently iterative. The discipline of the study requires that those conducting it pursue questions methodically and rigorously until there are no further questions to ask. This exhaustive, formal process is not conducive to quick fixes, and a committed management may be called on to protect the effectiveness of the study team's work by ensuring it the time needed to explore the process in question thoroughly.

The process capability effort at the Oklahoma City Works received a lot of help from a statistical software package called PCAP (Process Characterization Analysis Package). This predictive tool is an integrated collection of statistical techniques designed to aid engineers in obtaining thorough characterizations of complex processes. Using data collected during the normal course of production, testing, and performing many of the judgments of a statistician, PCAP allows engineers to identify the significant process variables systematically, the interactions among them, and their operating regions for maximum yields. It was used to characterize every manufacturing process in the plant and provided valuable insights into the capabilities of those processes.

Process control chart. This chart is a graphic display of the patterns and control limits of an industrial process, and when used as a tool to monitor a manufacturing process continually, it can provide a quick indication of a problem.

The chart displays control limits on a particular process in terms of specific characteristics. Such a characteristic might be the condition of a sampled circuit pack: does it work, or does it not work? A sample of circuit packs is inspected for the salient characteristic, and the number of packs sampled is divided into the number of defects. The resultant value is then plotted on the chart on which the X axis is time and the Y axis is some measure of the characteristic.

If a series of plots generates a random pattern, and if none of the plots is beyond the control limits, then the process is said to be in statistical control. If these conditions are not fulfilled, however, some cause or complex of causes is operating to degrade the quality of the product and must be found and corrected.

126

There are a number of different kinds of process control charts, but they all use a mean value derived from a process capability study to establish and control limits. The better the process, the better the value of the mean tends to be, and the lower the defect level, with zero as an ideal target. If a process chart shows a process in control, the only way the quality can be improved is to change the process.

The charts are used to measure the statistical behavior of each operation on a line, and the operator can use the chart to identify opportunities for improving the manufacturing process.

Statistical designed experiments. This is a statistical technique for comparing process variables and determining their significance. Its chief advantage is that it makes it possible to determine the best operating conditions of the process.

In one such experiment, the predictive statistical tool PCAP was used to analyze the wave soldering process used in making circuit packs for the 5ESS switch and AT&T 3B computers. In the wave soldering process, data were collected on a pack-by-pack basis to determine how selected parameters affect the associated defects. With carefully refined sampling techniques, this information was entered interactively into the PCAP package. In this way the soldering process was analyzed thoroughly.

Computations carried out by PCAP identified optimum process parameters such as conveyor speed, flux density, preheat temperature, solder temperature, and wave height. Additionally, the relationship between solder defects and several nonprocess related variables, such as printed circuit board or component lead solderability, were also determined through PCAP results.

Statistical inspection plans. These are formal methodologies for examining a specific quantity of product, and they serve as a basis for action with respect to that product. They were used to ensure that both internal and external suppliers of components were meeting the plant's quality standards. Furthermore, they helped identify suppliers who were providing parts that were causing problems and negatively affecting yields.

There are less costly alternatives to statistical inspection, but it was deemed necessary to bring some processes under statistical control, even to the point of conducting lot-by-lot screenings. The use of this type of inspection is an example of what became known as "doing it wrong (in terms of cost savings)" to ensure high quality in the products going to customers. The philosophy behind the slogan was simple: The Oklahoma City Works would take whatever quality measures were necessary to meet its customers' requirements. This included solving some problems "wrong" until there was time to implement the "right" solutions.

A product-oriented inspection system was not the ultimate solution, and while it helped ensure high quality, it did so at a very high price. What was needed was an approach that improved the process itself. Once a systems-engineered process capable of meeting customer specifications was implemented, quality could be *built* into the product rather than inspected into the product. At Oklahoma City, the Quality Maximization Plan, QUALMAX, provided a check and balance to ensure that quality problems are detected and corrected at the earliest possible stage of the process.

Beyond Basics

Quality maximization plan. This plan is executed at all points throughout a process by process checkers who report to the operating organization. The result is quick identification of problems, and an emphasis on the process rather than on the product.

If statistical inspections are carried out by a quality inspection group that does its work at the end of the line, the completed product must be sorted or screened to make the necessary fixes. This is an expensive process for several reasons. Workers downstream from the point at which a defect is introduced may invest considerable labor in a defective product. If a defect is not discovered early in the process, the necessary repairs may damage the product in some other way. And if the defect is not discovered before shipment, the customer finds the problem and the manufacturer incurs considerable repair costs plus the inestimable cost that goes with losing a customer's goodwill.

Process checking aims to avoid these costs by identifying defects early and by focusing on the process that caused the defects. If the process is of high quality, then it follows that the product will be too.

Process control tends to drive responsibility for quality to the people who do the work. If a problem is found, they work with the process checker to find the source. Is the operator using the correct documentation? Is the machine properly calibrated and set up? This approach also offers another potential cost savings: The more reliable the process, the less money need be spent for rigorous inspections at the end of the line.

This is not to say, of course, that endpoint inspection can be eliminated completely. In fact, it has an important check-and-balance role to play in the process-oriented quality scheme. If the inspectors at the end of the line discover a process is statistically out of control, it is their prerogative to shut the line down. However, these inspections need not be as detailed — or costly — when process control is working.

Design for manufacture. The quality improvement effort at the Oklahoma City Works has demonstrated some significant gains through increased interaction between the people who manufacture products and the product and component designers.

First, the design of a product directly affects the plant's ability to manufacture it to quality specifications. Process capability studies revealed, for example, that the plant was incapable of achieving required levels given the designs of certain products. The solution was a product redesign.

"If you have a dual-in-line integrated circuit package with 10 wires on a side, there's a way to orient that package so that you don't get solder bridges," former engineering director Larry Seifert explained. "Designers need to know that, and the best people to tell them are those involved with the manufacture of the package."

Designers also need to be aware of how their design changes in existing circuit packs will affect the manufacturing process. A number of small changes introduced separately can disrupt the complex flow of products through the factory. And, of course, designs that are impractical in a manufacturing sense also create problems.

To deal with these and related concerns, the management of the Oklahoma City Works aggressively pursued a design for manufacture effort with Bell Labs. Underlying the more formal aspects of the new relationship was the emphasis on teamwork that Seifert discussed earlier. Both plant and laboratory managers worked to focus their attention on the problems at hand, rather than wasting time assigning blame, fostering a more relaxed atmosphere for two-way communication.

"If you're in a cooperative mode with the designers, it's easier for them to involve manufacturing engineers in early work with a new technology, which gives you a chance to test it in the plant," Seifert explained. "That puts you ahead of the game."

Concrete steps also were taken. Bell Labs engineers were assigned to the plant to provide liaison and to be on hand to help solve problems quickly. Engineers from the Oklahoma City Works reviewed plans to redesign circuit packs, with an eye toward manufacturability. (One such review of a connector redesign saved an estimated $1.5 million in annual manufacturing costs.) Moreover, Seifert personally reviewed many of the proposed design changes with his engineers. And Bell Labs began sending design changes to Oklahoma City in manageable "bundles," when possible.

Simulations. Traditionally, labor has accounted for most of the costs in producing a product — far more than have materials. However, at the capital-intensive, highly automated Oklahoma City Works, this relationship has been reversed. On the 5ESS switch lines, for example, material now accounts for a large majority of the cost. As a result, the plant's entire manufacturing strategy must be changed. Computer simulations are invaluable tools for guiding and motivating that change.

Simulations have repeatedly shown that in many cases it is preferable to have people (labor) idle rather than carrying excess inventory (material costs.) Because of the complexity of the manufacturing process, this kind of revelation often is not intuitively obvious. It takes the power of a computer to balance the multiplicity of costs involved with setup, use of floor space, occasional idleness of workers, inventory, and so forth, to determine optimum operating conditions.

Experience has also demonstrated another fact that may not be intuitively obvious: Knowing something needs to be fixed is no assurance that it will be. In the quality improvement process, motivation is as important as know-how, and computer simulations help supply that motivation. They do it by graphically displaying the penalties that accrue to failure to change, while explicitly stating the economic benefits that attend change.

Computer simulations also have played a key role in specially designed continuous on-line manufacturing operations. Called CIM lines, these facilities use automatic machines and a computer-controlled flow of materials to achieve high-volume, high-quality yields. The CIM lines also rely on just-in-time delivery of materials, a practice that shrinks inventories by delivering the goods as they are needed, rather than stockpiling them on the factory floor.

Success mode analysis. This is not only an approach to identifying quality strengths in the plant, but is representative of a galaxy of attitudes and philosophies that emphasize the positive.

Success mode analysis strives to identify the factors that bring high quality to an operation or product. It is a way of evaluating both high-level processes and low-level ones to determine their strengths, with an eye to capitalizing on them elsewhere, when possible.

While it complements failure mode analysis, which seeks to find out why a problem occurred, it also plays down the negative aspects of quality management, with far-reaching ramifications. For example, Basey constantly stressed that it is good to find problems, since that is the first step in fixing them. It has also become a tenet of faith that once a problem is found, it — and not the organization or person with which it is associated — will be attacked. "We try not to waste time pointing fingers," one manager said. "We tend to look ahead, not behind."

Director's quality meeting. One of the places Basey and his people had an opportunity to put their positive philosophies into practice was at the Tuesday morning director's quality meeting. The first half of the session was devoted to status reports. When problems were identified, they were placed on an action register assiduously and discussed in the second half of the meeting, the portion devoted to finding solutions to problems. The purpose of these meetings was to provide a mechanism for anyone to bring any problem before the management team and get help.

"Two things especially impressed me about those meetings," Seifert said. "First was the attitude of helpfulness that prevailed. We weren't there to place blame, but to help fix problems. Second, when a problem was broached, it was religiously tracked. We had a secretary come into those meetings to do just that."

Quality assurance program for outside suppliers. Early in the quality improvement effort at Oklahoma City, it was recognized that the products going out the door could not be of high quality unless components coming into the plant were equally good. There also proved to be a problem with critical information provided by suppliers. Mistakes were found in orders and in design information. As Seifert put it, "We realized more than half the problems came from the outside."

To address these issues, plant employees now work more closely with suppliers, visiting their manufacturing facilities and analyzing their quality standards. They also have arranged for some suppliers of kit materials for just-in-time delivery, even on a daily basis.

When some suppliers of integrated circuits had difficulty meeting the plant's quality and reliability specifications, the Oklahoma City Works set up a so-called "IC upgrade area" to ensure that the components were up to specifications. Components coming into the factory from these suppliers were screened in the upgrade area, and those that failed to fulfill the necessary criteria were rejected.

Factory representative program. Under this program, an engineer or some other professional from the plant is assigned responsibility for seeing that a 5ESS switching office is delivered and installed on time. Under this arrangement, the factory representative serves as a liaison and advocate for the customer and installer, working within the plant to bring the needed resources to bear. For example, the representative might help procure materials needed for installation or track down essential documents. There are more than 100 people involved in the program, and they meet periodically to compare notes. Customer response to the program has been enthusiastic.

Customer involvement. Customers are an integral part of the quality improvement effort at the Oklahoma City Works. For example, Bell Communications Research, Inc., or Bellcore, the centralized technical support organization for some of AT&T's largest customers — the Bell operating companies — has a well-established presence at the plant. Bellcore conducts periodic quality process analyses, which evaluate the major elements of quality plans. Bellcore representatives join plant personnel in frequent reliability meetings and evaluate the product on-site.

As a part of its marketing thrust, the plant also has established a separate quality organization to plan and maintain an active customer visitation program. Such visits not only enhance communications between marketing, the plant, and the organizations that purchase its products, but allow customers to see firsthand the personal commitment to quality and customer satisfaction that exists there. For these reasons, the customer visitation program has proven to be an effective sales tool.

Summary

The Oklahoma City Works is an example of how quality is being redefined commensurate with changes in the company's practices, values, and objectives. The result is a concept of quality that puts it at the heart of the business. It is essential to customer satisfaction and an integral part of the company's product realization process. It is as much a concern of the product designer, the development engineer, the marketing planner, the salesperson, and the production engineer, as it is that of the quality control inspector on the line.

The Oklahoma City experience demonstrates what a skillful management team can do in a few years if it embraces this philosophy of quality and leads the rest of the organization in pursuit of it. The results can be a dramatic increase in the quality of products and a precipitous decline in costs. Moreover, both productivity and production output can be expanded greatly.

At the Oklahoma City Works, these results did not come easily, nor were they free. They required a significant investment in capital and the personal commitment of thousands of employes. Yet the return has been enormous, both in terms of the bottom line and in employee morale and commitment to company goals.

Appendix IV – Hewlett-Packard Company

Teamwork Is more Easily Praised than Practiced

In his keynote speech at the 39th Annual Quality Congress, John Young, president and chief executive officer of Hewlett-Packard Company, addressed the quality benefits of building teamwork. An article based on the speech appeared originally in the August 1985 issue of Quality Progress *magazine.*

In the late 1970s Hewlett-Packard grappled with some changes in our business environment. Cost was becoming an increasingly important consideration to our customers as we moved more and more into the computer business. International competition was heating up — especially the challenge from Japan and other nations of the Pacific Rim. Finally and most importantly, our customers were expecting more from us in the way of quality.

At that time we had an excellent reputation for quality. In fact, we led many a poll in that category. Yet we decided to address those first two changes — cost and international competition — by aiming at quality.

Our own internal survey showed us that fully 25 percent of Hewlett-Packard's manufacturing costs were involved in responding to quality problems — that is, not doing things right the first time. So in 1979 I asked that our field failure rates be cut to one-tenth their current levels by the end of the 1980s.

Why ask for a factor-of-ten improvement? If I'd called for an improvement of only 30 percent or so, people wouldn't have done anything until 1988. They wouldn't have been forced to radically rethink their operating procedures. They would have continued in what we call the "same old way," which we abbreviate with the initials of S-O-W: sow. Pictures of fat, ugly pigs are all over Hewlett-Packard, so I guess I got my point across.

We started the quality idea moving by sending a sizable group of key functional managers to — where else? — Japan. Our joint venture there, Yokogawa-Hewlett-Packard — we call it YHP — had already begun a total quality control campaign. The results were becoming visible.

YHP's efforts won it the esteemed Deming prize in 1982. During the five years it strove for that award, YHP cut manufacturing costs on its own products by 42 percent and inventory by 64 percent. Failure rates went down by 60 percent and R&D cycle time was cut by more than a third. At the same time, productivity almost doubled, and profits and market share improved by about a factor of three.

Our team's visit with YHP and other Japanese companies convinced them that there was a lot of room for improvements here in the States and that the potential paybacks were enormous. Our people came back and started some projects. Everywhere around Hewlett-Packard, quality teams sprang up. We felt they were an appropriate vehicle to tackle the quality challenge, and they fit in well with Hewlett-Packard's management style.

Today we have a lot of success stories to tell. Our field failure rates have been decreasing more than 20 percent a year. In fact, many parts of our business will meet my factor-of-ten goal in less than 10 years. Those successes have translated into bottom-line results. Let me cite just a few to give you an idea of their magnitude.

Our successes in manufacturing encouraged us to move the total quality control (TQC) concept across the entire organization. For example, we've improved the quality of our order processing. We now do a much better job of entering, filling, and billing orders. So now our customers pay us more promptly, and that shows in accounts receivable. In 1978, they averaged 62 days outstanding. Today, accounts receivable are down to an average of 54 days. Those improvements alone represent a savings of more than $100 million to the Hewlett-Packard Company.

We've also worked closely with our vendors to make sure they provide us quality parts. We invite them in, expose them to a quality seminar, and they get bit by the bug. The president of one of our suppliers came out of a five-day training session and sent the following message to his own regional managers: "If you don't find a need for this training and its application, you may be working for the wrong company." I may quibble with the style, but not the message.

Now you'd think that with such dramatic bottom-line results and more than 1,000 quality teams, we at Hewlett-Packard might feel pretty smug about our progress. We don't.

Last year we had a task force reappraise our quality team program. It concluded that our results were mixed. We hadn't yet succeeded in fully institutionalizing total quality control. In some parts of the company, quality was still a program. We'd rather it be a way of life.

The task force decided to try to identify what factors led to successful quality teams, and I thought you might be interested in what they learned. First, successful quality teams were fully integrated into their group's business strategy. They weren't just viewed as ancillary employee development exercises. Instead, they were considered as vehicles for pursuing major strategic objectives.

There's an interesting and subtle corollary here. The most successful teams operated within an environment where continuous quality improvement was the paramount goal. It's easy to focus on other, seemingly more immediate goals — such as getting those shipments out the door. When you get in that mindset, quality can be relegated easily to the bottom of the priority list.

I don't have any easy answer for the dilemma — I want shipments out the door, too. Yet a strong commitment to improving the process is the only way to counterbalance the pressures of the short term. What is required, then, is what one of our divisions calls a constancy of purpose — a belief that pursuing quality *is* the best way to get those shipments out the door.

The second factor that successful quality teams all had in common was what we call management ownership. I don't mean management support; I mean ownership. Let me explain the difference.

When we first started quality teams, we limited management's involvement. We gave teams responsibility for choosing the problems they'd work on. Management's role was to stay out of the way. That hands-off approach works fine if all employees know exactly what their work-group's objectives are and how they fit in a broader organizational context. In a complex and rapidly changing business environment, that can't always be the case.

Where quality teams at Hewlett-Packard have been successful, managers have been closely involved. They used quality teams as a resource for accomplishing their business objectives. And they practiced what they preached.

The third requirement for successful teams was training: training in problem solving, statistics, team building, and process analysis. That last one — process analysis — has been the most difficult for our people to master. Considering all work as a "process" has been a difficult conceptual hurdle. We've found that many people are unable to fully characterize the very processes they use, and we're hard at work building a new set of skills here.

The fourth and final factor that has contributed to successful quality teams was teamwork. That's always been a management style we've prided ourselves on — an integral part of "the Hewlett-Packard way" from the beginning. So you'll be surprised — as we were — at our discovery that we still had a lot to learn. We found that, while we've always honored the spirit of teamwork, we haven't always practiced it in a structured and professional way. We assumed it would happen automatically.

Of course it was in quality teams where the issue first cropped up. It became quite clear after they began operating that many of their participants didn't have the conceptual and personal skills needed to make them work.

This same perception became more clear as we moved to just-in-time manufacturing. It lays bare the bones of a group dynamic. There was simply no slack to cover up a team's glitches or slow spots.

Our increased awareness of how important it is to systematically pursue teamwork stems from another consideration. That's the increased size of the

Hewlett-Packard organization and the growing interdependence of our more than 53 different product divisions. At the beginning of this decade, Hewlett-Packard had 52,000 employees. Today we have more than 83,000. By the end of the decade, we'll top 140,000. We still operate as one company, and that's a big team to get moving in the same direction.

We're also moving more and more into the systems business, where we provide customers with total solutions that include hardware and software from sometimes as many as 10 different divisions. It's a teamwork challenge of immense proportions.

So let me take the very broad view and discuss some of the issues we're considering as we try to institutionalize quality and teamwork across the entire Hewlett-Packard organization. I'll approach this subject from the perspective of what I view as some of the prerequisites for organization-wide teamwork.

The first requirement has to be consensus on goals. We at Hewlett-Packard have a set of seven corporate objectives that range from achieving enough profit to finance our own growth, to defining the fields of interest we will pursue, to describing the way we want to manage ourselves. These guidelines were first written in 1957, and in aggregate they define how we intend to grow and profit over the years. They have guided many a corporate decision.

We've also worked hard to make sure that the personal interests of our employees are in line with the company's goals. We have two major incentive programs that help accomplish this. The first is profit-sharing among all employees, where everyone gets the same percentage of base salary as a bonus. The amount people receive depends on our profitability, and that really helps get everyone in the organization pulling in the same direction.

We also have an employee stock purchase plan, where the company contributes one dollar for every three an employee puts in. More than three fourths of our people participate in the plan. The result has been that, since our people own part of the company, they also feel ownership for some of the company's problems.

That umbrella of consensus provides an important backdrop for a difficult step, which is to achieve congruence of goals among all of an organization's subdivisions.

In my view, the best way to do this is to keep the focus on customers and to define both objectives and quality from their point of view. Satisfying them is the only reason we're in business.

It's easy to get internally driven — to adopt structures and procedures that make us comfortable. Let me give you an example. Until last summer, Hewlett-Packard was organized according to product lines. We had a sales force for instruments and another for computers. We asked for teamwork from both to meet customer needs for total solutions from us that required pieces from all parts of the organization. The efforts were sincere, but the organizational hurdles too great. Our solution was a major reorganization.

Today we're organized along market lines, with all the pieces — hardware, software, sales, and support — combined to meet the needs of the market they serve. The result has made teamwork much easier to achieve.

I've said that the first two prerequisites for organization-wide teamwork are consensus on goals and the correct alignment of the organization to pursue them effectively. A third prerequisite for teamwork is a thorough understanding of the process by which we pursue our business goals and the roles we play in it. The more broadly you can view that process, the better.

Last year our computer support operation had a quality project that illustrates the benefits of the broad view. This group is responsible for supplying repair parts and exchange assemblies for all our computers worldwide. Until last year, they had a less than enviable reputation with *their* customers, who are Hewlett-Packard's field sales engineers. Their response time just wasn't fast enough. So they used TQC to identify the cause of their slowness.

They found that 85 percent of their delay was waiting for just 20 percent of the parts they needed — and that those parts, in turn, came from other Hewlett-Packard divisions. So they put on an educational road show that they took around the company. It mapped the entire process of repairing customer orders — from customer, to Hewlett-Packard sales engineer, to computer support operation, back to other Hewlett-Packard divisions. This broad picture convinced the other divisions that they were part of a very broad and important process. Because they're more aware of the important role they play, they now do a much better job of supplying the computer support operation with parts.

That broad perspective on quality leads to a fourth organizational issue, and a thorny one. Performance measurements and reward systems have to facilitate the cross-functional and cross-divisional teamwork that makes quality possible.

One of our quality managers tells a story that illustrates this well. One day he was acting as facilitator for two different groups of buyers, and they were identifying quality problems to work on. Each group came up with a list of 100 of them.

This facilitator's background was in production. So he was amazed that neither list of 100 problems identified late parts as a problem. From the vantage point of production, that was quality problem number one. So he asked one of the supervisors in purchasing why they hadn't identified late parts as a problem. The reply: "Because we don't get measured or evaluated on them."

The overriding importance of performance measures and their effect on teamwork has caused some careful reappraisal at Hewlett-Packard. On the individual level, our employee evaluation forms have been revised to better emphasize quality and teamwork. Our recruiters are looking for that personal skill as essential for new hires, too.

Hewlett-Packard's new ranking system for quality managers is another example of changing a reward system to better reflect quality and teamwork goals. We used to rank quality managers primarily on the number of people in their organization. That system rewarded them for building empires, which is the opposite of what you want if you're going to institutionalize quality and make it everybody's business.

Today a Hewlett-Packard quality manager gets rated on a much broader set of criteria, including complexity of the organization and cross-divisional linkages. They're motivated to create teams with other departments and to involve a wide range of people in quality efforts. Quality assurance managers at Hewlett-Packard are on their way to becoming facilitators and change masters, not policemen and administrators.

On the organizational level, we're still grappling with the question. We're aware that not all Hewlett-Packard divisions can be measured with the same performance yardstick. For example, there are very different expense and revenue patterns for software and hardware. Software can leverage some of our hardware efforts, yet we have no way of defining or rewarding the contribution software makes to hardware sales. I bring up the issue not because we've got the solution — we're working on it — but to illustrate the very real challenge of getting quality goals, measurements, and rewards correctly aligned.

The final requirement for successful teamwork has to be an organization's management style. Do managers view their employees as their customers? Are they good listeners? Do they encourage honest feedback? Are they willing to compromise? Do they value consensus? Are they willing to invest the time it takes to create it? These and scores of other questions reflect the vast gulf between management theory and practice. They also reflect how essential it is that managers model the very behavior they want to encourage.

Let me summarize:

- First, quality teams need to be closely integrated into strategic business goals.
- Second, managers must "own" the teams as a vehicle to achieve those goals.
- Third, the teams must be thoroughly equipped with the skills and tools needed to get the job done.
- Finally, the teams must operate within an organizational and cultural environment that encourages teamwork.

At Hewlett-Packard, we often call our quality people "change masters." That's what I invite you to be, and my best wishes accompany you as you make the quality revolution an American institution.

Appendix V – IBM

IBM's Total Quality Improvement System

Edward J. Kane
Director of Quality
IBM Corporation
Purchase, New York

Introduction

IBM refers to its quality management system as *Total Quality Improvement*. It is called *total* because it is not limited to any specific area, but applies to all functions and areas of the business. *Quality* is the essence of the system. It is critical to the achievement of IBM's business goals for the 1980s. It must be well-defined and become a way of life for all employees. Its focus is on *improvement* because of IBM's firm belief that the best approach is to develop a system that continuously improves the quality of every product, service, and work activity in the company.

Quality improvement at IBM came about as a rededication to excellence. It involves and requires a permanent commitment by line management to improve the effectiveness (performing the right actions), efficiency (performing actions correctly), and adaptability (meeting the changing needs of the business) of every process and activity through which the resources of the business are managed.

We recognize that quality cannot exist for long simply as an emphasis program. Quality improvement must be accepted by the line organization as its responsibility, and it must be imbedded into the fabric of the management system.

History of Quality at IBM

The rededication to excellence started in 1980, but it had its foundation in an already existing base. It began in 1914 with Thomas J. Watson, Sr., and IBM's predecessor company, the Computing-Tabulating-Recording Company. Mr. Watson had strong beliefs and made them operational during his tenure as IBM's chief executive officer.

Thomas J. Watson, Jr., who succeeded Mr. Watson, Sr., as chief executive officer, first articulated IBM's three basic beliefs. They have guided IBM's business conduct ever since:

- Respect for the individual.
- The best customer service of any corporation in the world.
- The belief that all tasks can be accomplished in a superior fashion.

Respect for the individual is the basis for much of IBM's ongoing management education and is reinforced by many practices and programs throughout the company. Participative management, which is essential to IBM's quality effort, flows from respect for the individual. Providing the best customer service and believing that all tasks can be accomplished in a superior fashion represent the excellence value on which IBM bases its quality management system.

Recent chief executice officer, John R. Opel, articulated IBM's goals for the 1980s:

- To grow with the industry.
- To exhibit product leadership across our entire product line — to excel in technology, value, and quality.
- To be the most efficient in everything we do — to be the low-cost producer, the low-cost seller, and the low-cost administrator.
- To sustain our profitability, which funds our growth.

Growth, however, introduces change which must be managed and nurtured. Quality must be designed and built in, not added on; therefore, changes in thinking and attitude must occur as well. Improving efficiency and driving out errors at their origin is essential but not sufficient. Little is accomplished if we work mightily to finely hone processes which are obsolete. All process by which the resources of the business are managed must be continuously adapted to meet the changing needs of the business.

To be the best competitor requires efficiency in every area. In turn, this mandates not only capital investment but superior job design and people management. In the end, profitability depends in great part on motivated people, low overhead structures, and cost effective, defect-free process which are able to adapt to the changing needs of the business in a timely and orderly way. The key to the achievement of goals is through effective quality management.

IBM's current chief executive officer, John F. Akers, like his predecessors, is enthusiastic about the importance of quality. He also understands the need for the consistent and constant practice of excellence. In a speech to the American Electronics Association in 1984 he said, "We have made some real strides. . .but quality is something you have to work at every day. The moment we start to relax is the moment we fall short of the ideal." More recently in a letter in *THINK* magazine he said, ". . .so the push for quality continues. It's not only that we have no other choice, it's that we wouldn't have it any other way."

The Need

Haven't IBM people and products always enjoyed a reputation for excellence? Why, then, is quality emphasis needed? At IBM, there are three reasons:

1. *Changing customer needs and expectations.* Today, data processing systems operate at the heart of business enterprise. Our large systems users want our excellent service if they must have service, but they would prefer no service at all. At the other end of the scale in personal computers, terminals, and workstations, the user is not a data processing professional and wants a friendly system which is available all the time. All information systems users have clear requirements, namely ease of use and high systems reliability and availability.

2. *Competition.* In the information processing industry, competition is intense. Our competitors have high reliability products and high hopes for greater market share, and the quality emphasis is seen all over the world. IBM means to keep its leadership position and, therefore, must constantly improve toward defect-free goals, never accepting "good" performance. At IBM quality is seen as the competitive edge, an equal partner with performance and price.

3. *The high cost of nonquality.* Many people believe that it costs something to produce high quality — hiring good people, training them well, superior job and process design, good procedures and tools, etc. The point is debatable because all of these things represent an investment to prevent errors and defects. In addition, the payback tends to be both high and immediate.

Clearly, it costs even more to produce poor quality because we must fix products and processes that do not conform to the need that created them. Costs for inspection, scrap, rework, warranty claims, mistakes in coding, typing errors, etc., often dwarf the original cost to product.

The "art" of fixing often creates additional defects which must be corrected. Further, if the fixing is not aimed at permanent process improvement rather than single event problem solving, the result will be to throw people and money at the problem. And every time this is done, the process producing the defect and the company become a little less competitive.

Fixing problems in the customer office is not only expensive for IBM but also for IBM's customer, the focal point of the quality effort. As already discussed, disruption of the customer's business violates the principles of effective quality management and is, therefore, unacceptable.

Quality Concepts

IBM has developed five basic concepts which are embodied in the quality improvement plans of all its organizational units:

1. *Quality improvement results from management action.* Executive management must lead, inspire, and involve itself in the quality effort or that effort will be short-lived. Only positive action by senior management will provide the answers; words alone will not. The following is a list of the actions taken by IBM's senior management:

- A formal quality policy.
- Several quality specific corporate instructions.
- A corporate-wide quality organization.
- A management review structure from the top down.
- Top to bottom quality education.
- Supplier quality programs.
- The use of the reward structure to recognize quality achievement.
- Communications plans for quality.
- Quality improvement plans in all areas.
- Quality specific items in individual performance plans, as well as in operating, business area, and strategic plans.

The continuous review, testing, and assessment of results by management will demonstrate the seriousness and permanence of the quality movement. IBM top management, starting with the chief executive officer, not only supported the quality movement but involved themselves as key players in it. Most importantly, in involving themselves, they added value to the concept and contributed to its implementation.

2. *Everyone must be involved.* It is critical in quality improvement to achieve not only clarity in person-to-person communications, but that a new sense of group interaction on problems and improvement of work activity take place. IBM defines quality for itself in a simple way: meeting the requirements of customers with defect-free products and services. The most important customer to any individual employee will be the person who receives his or her work product. The objective is to neither pass on defective work nor accept it. Once an individual accepts defective work, he or she owns it and has the responsibility to fix it. This customer/supplier relationship has been a powerful tool in changing the way people think about their work activities.

Quality improvement teams (including quality circles) are used widely at IBM with emphasis on continuous improvement, where management directs the activity of the team and provides training and management support. Generally, there is management selection of participants as well as voluntary involvement. The reason for getting everyone involved, of course, is a matter of simple mathematics. If direct manufacturing employees are the only ones involved, the potential is limited to 10 percent of the people and 10 percent of the benefit. In IBM, where there are currently 395,000 employees, if everyone can be involved and each removes defects from his or her work product that saves just $1,000 a year, the company would save $395 million. In order to generate $395 million in profit, it would take $2.66 billion of additional revenue. This illustrates the potential of quality, through defect removal, driving productivity.

3. *Focus for improvement must be on the job process.* Dedicated commitment to goal achievement and inspired people management is a discipline that is second nature to IBM employees. Quality management, however, added a new dimension of continuous improvement to excellence in these areas. The concept, "Focus on the Process," can be simply stated but implementation requires new forms of discipline and great attention to detail.

In describing focus on the process or process management, the analogy is drawn to people management, a concept already well-understood and practiced in IBM, (see Figure 1).

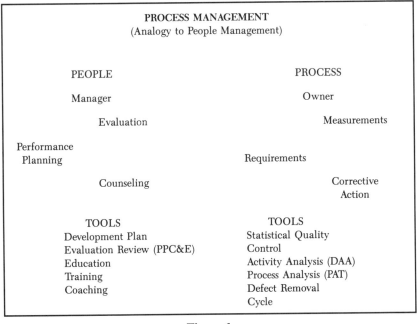

Figure 1

The idea is that effective management of human resources is accomplished through periodic and joint planning of the performance expected of the employee (long cycle). This is followed by continuous communication, evaluation, and counseling (shorter cycle). As expectations become accomplishments, performance plans are updated by manager and employee, setting new goals to be achieved, and the shorter cycle repeats.

145

Process management uses a similar cycle but deals with the manager's (or employee's) relationship with his or her work activity. Before anything sensible can be accomplished, there must be an owner (analogous to manager) identified who has responsibility to make the work activity productive. Next the owner must understand the customer requirements to which he or she must conform (analogous to performance planning). This is the longer cycle and is also periodically revisited.

Once requirements are understood, measurements can be established to test conformance and corrective action taken. This is the shorter cycle which is analogous to evaluation and counseling people. It, in turn, gives rise to a revised requirements cycle, etc.

The analogy is a simple one but because of managers' general comfort with people management, it has been useful in gaining acceptance with process management. All managers, for example, spend 40 hours every year in management development courses, most of which deal with people management, i.e., participative management and techniques for making the human resource more productive. The cycle described, therefore, is not only well-understood but continuously executed and measured.

In 1980, IBM began focusing on IBM products and manufacturing processes. By the end of 1981, IBM had achieved worldwide involvement and significant benefits accrued both in terms of improved quality and productivity. Several examples are included at the end of this paper for illustrative purposes. Building on the product processes, we turned our attention to the nonproduct areas. Two examples involve marketing and administration.

The first example, in the marketing area, involves the generation of special bids to customers upon which depended the successful closing of large amounts of revenue. The process of bid proposal, approval, and delivery to customers typically required a 90-day cycle. The sales force reasoned that if cycle time was reduced to 30 days, its ability to sell new business would greatly improve.

A divisional vice president was designated as the process owner. The key indicators selected for measurement and tracking were response time to customers and the percentage of bids closed versus the total offered (bid close rate). The existing process was defined and documented, and bottlenecks (defects) were analyzed. This was followed by the systematic chipping away at removal of the inhibitors to a free-flowing special bids process. Actions were taken, such as reducing the number of decision points, delegating greater authority to the field organization, and eliminating delay by automating the data collection and approval process. The results over a 24-month period show clear improvement, reducing the approval cycle to an average of 15 days. Even more significant, the bid closing rate improved from 20 percent to 65 percent over that same period.

The second example, in the administrative area, involves an established field measurement system on a composite of business controls indicators. Examples include backlog asset management and accounts receivable. The comparison rankings showed one region continuously in last place on a monthly basis having never met its established goals. Region management decided to take a process view in an attempt to reverse the poor showing in business controls.

A quality project team was established. Two region line managers were dedicated to the team as co-chairmen. One manager represented marketing and the other, administration. Team members were selected from branch, region, and division offices and represented all functions.

An evaluation and analysis of "Theories of Causes" determined that the dominant cause of the controls problem resided in the accounts receivable area. This area was then evaluated as to its dominant causes, and action plans were directed to the removal of those causes.

Three significant actions were taken. First, an additional allocation of college "new hires" was deployed to the order entry process to improve billing quality through error (incorrect orders) removal. Second, education and training programs were implemented to raise the knowledge and awareness level of branch personnel. Finally, a program was established to improve communication to better define and clarify the requirements of customers. This program included such items as confirmation letters for orders, special mailings to clarify special terms and conditions, and customer seminars to clarify pricing, financing alternatives, and new terms and conditions.

After one year, the region met its total delinquency measurement for the first time in history. Three months later, the region attained all four A/R measurements, which consisted of total delinquency, items over 90 days, total aged items, and six-month accounts, for the first time. Six months later, the region achieved a combined controls measurement (A/R Backlog/Asset Management) perfect score of "0" points. By comparison, the previous score was 2,500 points versus a division target of 600 for all regions.

Quality Focus on Business Process

IBM then turned its attention to the more complex, cross-functional processes. These were typified by fewer measurements and unknown limits, but represented an even greater opportunity for improvement and productivity gain. These cross-functional processes include order entry, billing, centralized accounts receivable, personnel data systems, inventory and materials management, distribution, production control, and procurement. These identified processes are cross-functional. That is, they are logically related but physically and organizationally dispersed. Without the identification of a person with clearly defined responsibility for the entire process, it is difficult to understand the capabilities or the failings of these cross-functional activities. If they could be better understood, simplified, and made adaptable to the needs of the business, it was reasoned that the resulting productivity gains would be immense.

A common understanding was needed, and it began with the definition of process, shown in Figure 2. The work done in any enterprise is part of a process and falls within this definition. In cross-functional processes anyone's work activity may be part of one or multiple processes. However, the organizational structure of most companies, including IBM, causes work to be managed vertically, that is, through organizations, units, or functions; processes flow horizontally across organizations and functions. Therefore, the more sharply we tend to focus on achievement of specific objectives and measurements within a specific function or organization, the more we encourage exactly what we are trying to avoid — suboptimization.

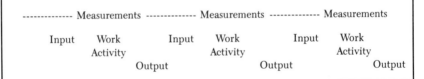

Process Definition

A group of logically related tasks (decisions and activities) that when performed, utilize the resources of the business to produce definitive results.

Processes are independent of organization and have the following characteristics:

- Measurable inputs
- Value added
- Measurable outputs
- Repeatable activity

------------- Measurements ------------- Measurements ------------- Measurements

| Input | Work Activity | Input | Work Activity | Input | Work Activity |
| | Output | | Output | | Output |

Figure 2

We are now seeking to foster optimization and adaptability across the entire process. Where the work activity is logically related but organizationally segmented, information processing is a key in making that activity productive. But information must be managed carefully just as any other resource to ensure that it, too, is not suboptimized within the process. Part of the IBM billing process is a good example (see Figure 3).

The billing consists of 14 major cross-functional activities which are logically related but physically dispersed among 255 marketing branches and 25 regional offices, a similar number of field service locations, and several headquarters operations and manufacturing sites. The work is cross-functional and nonsequential within any function. It is tied together by a complex information system. Overall, 96 percent of the invoices are accurate, but because of the high cost of adjusting those that are incorrect, 54 percent of the total resource was devoted to cost of quality. Some of that cost is for prevention and appraisal (98.5 percent of the invoices delivered to customers are correct), but most can be attributed to failure of some kind. This is testimony to the efficiencies of information systems and points to the great need to prevent errors rather than fix them after the fact. This example also highlights the opportunity for improvement with attendant savings in just one "white-collar" process.

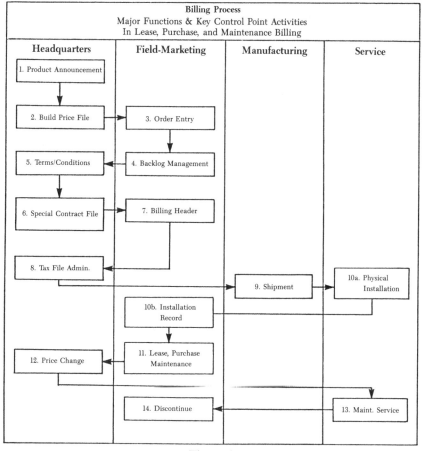

Figure 3

(This figure uses the PAT flow-diagram developed by Jan Nordstrom of IBM Sweden. Also see J. Carlisano, "Process Flow Analysis," *Quality*, December 1984, p.72.)

The first step in improving the billing process — or any other process — is to designate an owner, someone responsible for optimization across the entire work process. The owner is typically the manager most responsible for the results of the process. The owner of the billing process, for example, is the vice president of business systems, an executive directly responsible for most of the activities shown under "Headquarters" in Figure 3. This vice president holds a high-level position; however, he does not have responsibility for areas such as field marketing or manufacturing, as can be seen in Figure 3. Nevertheless, as process owner, the vice president is in a good position to cause changes to be made in these other areas. If a disagreement would arise about a change in one of the billing areas not reporting directly to the vice president, an escalation procedure would carry the matter to the next higher level of the corporation. At this point, the owner is the advocate for change in the process. The concurring area presents the case for maintaining the status quo; as a result of this proceeding, a decision is made. Because of the responsibility and authority given to the process owner, IBM does not anticipate that this escalation procedure will be used often.

Work is well underway at IBM to improve the billing process and — though work remains to be done in this widespread and complex process — important changes have already been seen in key billing quality measurements. By comparison, a relatively complex process that is largely confined to one unit can be improved more directly and expeditiously. In the billing example, changes were implemented at the functional and first-level management as well as employee levels (and eventually provided additional requirements for changes in the central billing process).

In 1980, the National Service Division, responsible for service on customer systems, adopted a policy of "error-free service" and began to focus on improving the service delivery process. The owner of this process was the vice president of service support, who reports directly to the president of the division. The earliest result of this concentration on improving the process was a singular finding: we were perceiving quality in a different manner than many of our customers, as shown by customer satisfaction surveys.

As a result of this analysis, a set of critical success factors essential to error-free service from the customer's viewpoint was developed. These included service dispatch response, total time from incident to fix, hardware repair time, software support, preventative maintenance program, availability of a trained field engineer, spare parts availability, telephone diagnostic capability, and technical back-up.

A measurement system incorporating the above factors and called the System for Service Quality (SSQ) was developed. The service "inhibitors," once identified, provide information on the nature of the root causes of problems and lead to the root cause removal. These solutions are implemented at the process level and are, therefore, permanent.

The process orientation which is provided by SSQ has allowed IBM to improve the quality of service as seen by the customer (the true measure of quality). At the same time, costs have been positively affected. Several SSQ studies have indicated that "error-free" service calls take only half the parts and one-third of the service time when compared to those with errors. Error-free service calls affect the customers as well. The length of service incident decreases, thereby increasing systems availability. The message has become very clear; when the service process is properly designed and carefully implemented, everyone benefits.

The changes made as a result of SSQ data are numerous and significant. Automated reporting methods, for example, provide real-time feedback on customer problems and reduce the cost of that feedback. The resulting improved service data analysis permits the removal of many of the causes of service inhibitors. These were achieved by improved dispatching methods, more precise training requirements, reorganization and assignment of service calls, increased investment in spare parts testing, and improved failure analysis methodologies.

The net result is an increase in the percentage of error-free calls taken every month. The measured progress is often slow, but the changes are significant because of their permanent nature.

The lessons to be learned in improving critical business processes are:
• Management commitment is essential.
• Success is long-term.
• A disciplined methodology is needed.
• Experimentation is beneficial.
• Error-oriented measurements at the task level must be employed.
• Focus must be on improving the process itself.

At IBM we are convinced that if this kind of participative and experimental environment is provided for all employees, the critical processes by which the resources of the business are managed will remain not only healthy but, more importantly, competitive and vitally relevant to their purpose.

Process Certification

It is important that the owner certify in some formal way the health and competitiveness of the process he or she manages. (This is conceptually analogous to certification by quality engineering that a tool or process will produce a desired result.) Processes do not naturally stay lean and competitive.

When meeting customer requirements is not the first consideration, attention turns to defensive protection of headcount, and budget preservation becomes more prevalent than creativity, experimentation, and investment in change. Improving the process by initiating change and supporting it with education and training, new tools, and better information and procedures helps overcome the tendencies of a process to grow fat and the management to become complacent. By requiring a process owner to certify the competitiveness of the process and holding the owner accountable for the output of the process, we bring the needed visibility to the true state of the process.

A strong belief in self-assessment plus outside audit has motivated IBM to institute the certification model illustrated in Figure 4. The process owner has the responsibility to rate process quality. In addition, the corporate audit function will selectively perform independent assessments on a similar basis, since self-inspection can never replace management inspection.

Process Certification

Categories

5. The process, as currently practiced, is ineffective; major exposures exist requiring expeditious corrective actions, or the basics of quality management are not in place.
4. The process, as currently practiced, may have some operational or control weaknesses which require corrective action, but the resulting exposures are containable, and the weaknesses can be corrected in the near future. The basics of quality management are in place.
3. The process as currently practiced is effective (meets the customer's requirements) and no significant operational inefficiencies or control exposures exist.
2. In addition to category 3 requirements, major improvements have been made to the process with tangible and measurable results realized. Environmental change is assessed with resulting process changes anticipated and committed (to meeting customer's future requirements).
1. In addition to category 2 requirements, the outputs of the process are assessed by the owner and the auditor from the customer viewpoint as being substantially defect-free (i.e., to the level the process caan reasonably deliver).

Notes

1. These descriptions are based on an IBM internal document; the author has made changes in that document for purposes of clarification.
2. The certification model refers to the "basics of quality management." For IBM, this refers to key factors which must be present in the process owner's quality plan. They are:

   • Ownership assigned.
   • Process/subprocess defined and documented.
   • Supplier/customer relationships and requirements identified.
   • Quality measurements and control points established.
   • Process simplification applied.
   • Defect prevention methodology and statistical methods utilized.

Figure 4

4. *No level of defect is acceptable.* Next, let's look within this process concept and describe more specifically how errors are removed from the work activity. The philosophy allows that people will make mistakes, which is acceptable, providing that we are unrelenting in finding and removing the cause of the error. This must be accomplished in a measured and disciplined manner.

Defect Removal Cycle

The IBM approach is to use a four-step cycle applied to each process segment.

The first step is to identify and establish grass roots measurements which are defect-oriented and, therefore, will be meaningful at the work activity level. Once the measurements have been established, any deviation identifies a defect or an error for analysis. The defects are then categorized using statistical methods and can be used to set priorities. Second, a determination is made as to the root cause of the defect. Third, alternative ways to eliminate the causes of the defect are generated. Finally, before a solution is implemented, the alternatives must be tested and evaluated against the specific pass/fail criteria established in the original measurements. If it works and is not a suboptimized solution, it is introduced into the process and new targets are established for the process.

5. *Quality improvement reduces total costs.* Estimates are made of all quality costs. These are the dollars IBM spends to ensure that its services and products meet customer requirements. It includes the dollars spent to rework things that do not meet requirements or to fix things that break. These expenditures are classified into two broad categories, cost of conformance and cost of nonconformance.

The costs of conformance include the prevention measures of selecting materials, education, training, procedures/systems, and tools, and the appraisal measures of performing audits, tests, assurance, and inspections. Together these add up to about 25 percent of total quality costs.

The costs of nonconformance or failure include all repair activity, scrap/rework, engineering changes, problem determination, warranty costs, etc. These relate primarily to manufacturing and product functions, but marketing and administration have their scrap and rework also. It comes in the form of deferred and cancelled orders, shipped and uninstalled systems, typing errors in letters and invoices, and accounting miscodes.

This is the major portion of quality costs, amounting to about 75 percent. Total quality costs range between 15 and 40 percent of the revenue stream depending on which factors are included. Our comparisons with other companies show that many companies have similar costs.

Spending more on prevention to improve the capabilities of process and using the defect removal cycle dramatically reduces failure costs, which in turn reduces overall quality costs and funds the increased prevention. The leverage in finding an error at its source versus waiting until it occurs in the field can be more than 100 to 1 in many cases.

Cost of quality analysis is used by IBM units on an informal voluntary basis but is encouraged because it can be useful in focusing management attention, establishing priorities for improvement, and monitoring progress over time.

After a good deal of study and experience, we believe that it is reasonable to reduce quality costs as a percent of revenue by half, providing a significant productivity gain as well as increased customer satisfaction. This will manifest itself in improved profitability, return to the customer in terms of reduced prices, and increased IBM competitiveness. For IBM, the opportunity is measured in billions of dollars a year as the quality benefits materialize. This, however, will only come as a by-product of disciplined and continuous quality improvement efforts. These efforts are being aggressively pursued, and although significant benefit has resulted, we believe that we are closer to the beginning than the end.

Summary

Productivity gain in general is realized by virtue of three factors — one, capital investment; two, improved job design; and three, superior people management. The concentration in this chapter has been primarily on improvement in job design and achieving higher levels of participation by all employees. It should be noted that, while often taken as a given in IBM, there has also been great emphasis on both capital investment and research and development in the late 1970s and again in the early 1980s. To remain an industry leader, IBM invests heavily in these areas.

It should also be restated that the IBM objective is not defect-free at any cost, but that the quality focus is applied consistently to reach the level of defect-free by removing failure cost and moving closer to the objective of being the most cost-effective in everything we do. The objective of adaptability — that is, the timely changing of process to meet business needs — must constantly be in mind since this is critical to remaining the industry leader for the long-term. This might mean that a process on its way to becoming defect-free is deliberately set back because the technology or process is altered significantly to achieve a capability breakthrough. But here the philosophy of continuous improvement takes hold once again, and efficiency is steadily raised.

It is clear that the responsibility for improving the business process in IBM rests clearly with line management. In the end, the line must take leadership and embed the quality focus into the management system so that it matures and becomes a way of life. The quality staff responsibility is in the ownership of the methodology. Specifically, the quality community must be certain that the proper tools and techniques are utilized effectively to help the process owner simplify, control, make more efficient, and meet the needs of the business.

If all can do their jobs in this way, the business processes will be well on their way to meeting the defect-free criteria envisioned.

Appendix VI – 3M

World Class Quality
The 3M Process for Improvement

Douglas N. Anderson
Director, Staff Quality
3M

Gaining the Edge With Quality

Quality has become one of the hot topics in business today. On the surface, quality improvement appears to be a dynamic new business tool of the 1980s. However, a closer look reveals that "Total Quality," the involvement of an entire business organization in an ongoing process of continuous improvement, has been with us for more than 30 years. But until recently, total quality was primarily a Japanese concept. Ironically, it was American business management experts who planted the seeds of total quality in Japan after World War II.

Since the war, the Japanese have used a total quality philosophy not only to rebuild their economy, but to move from an "also ran" position to a leadership role in many markets worldwide. The Japanese feat has clearly demonstrated the significance of quality as a competitive strategy. Japanese companies have become the dominant competitors in such industries as steel, automobiles, cameras, and electronics through unswerving application and leadership of the total quality improvement process. The most visible features of this tremendous transformation have been the growing numbers of Japanese products that are consistently more reliable than those of western competitors, and are marketed at a lower cost.

Invariably the question arises: What are they doing that we are not? Typical responses are:

- "The traditional work ethic of the Japanese."
- "Quality circles."
- "Lower pay scales."
- "A more positive business environment."
- "Kanban systems."

Although all of these answers have some merit, none explains Japan's success.

157

If we learn one thing from Japan, it should be that quality improvement depends on a systematic approach throughout the total organization. There are no quick solutions to quality. Rather, it must become a permanent, managed process that examines all products, procedures, and processes on a continuous basis for constant improvement.

Summarizing the concept is simple. Defining and implementing the process is a tremendous task.

3M's Beginning with Total Quality

3M's involvement in the total quality process began in 1979 when its top executives attended a series of seminars on organizational quality improvement. Top management under Lew Lehr, then 3M chief executive officer and chairman of the board, agreed that the improvement process should be adapted to 3M and, in 1980, established 3M's Corporate Staff Quality Department. The department was charged with the responsibility for defining quality objectives and designing a strategy to implement quality improvement throughout the corporation.

It began by adapting five essentials of quality as the basis for 3M's new quality philosophy. These are listed as follows:

1. *Management commitment.* The first and most important quality concept 3M has adopted is management commitment. This commitment must start at the top of the organization, where it must be recognized that quality improvement does not just happen, but rather must be planned and actively managed like every other aspect of the business if it is to become a way of life.

Experts believe that as much as 85 percent of all errors can be attributed to management failure — failure to provide the proper training, to properly define requirements, to take proper corrective action, and so on.

Management must take a leadership role in demonstrating commitment and cultivating that same attitude in every employee. The critical challenge is to create individual, personal quality commitments throughout the organization.

At 3M, the overall corporate improvement process is guided by a corporate Quality Steering Team, or QST. This team is made up of 3M's senior management. Together, the members of the corporate QST set corporate quality policy and define overall business objectives. In addition, each member works closely with the individual organizations to integrate quality measurements into their reporting systems.

2. *Quality is consistent conformance to customers' expectations.* In late 1980, Lew Lehr defined quality as consistent conformance to customers' expectations. There are two significant changes from what the others have said by using this definition. The word consistent implies doing it right every time rather than just doing it right the first time. The real paradigm shift is in

the use of the word expectations. By using terms such as "fitness for use" or "meeting requirements," most people want to revert to simply documenting the product specifications and continuing to meet them for a long period of time. They treat quality as if it were a static situation. Using words such as "requirements" or "specifications" leads many people to believe that quality is strictly product-oriented and does not involve most staff support people in the company. Using "expectations" as part of the definition automatically forces people in sales, marketing, billing, shipping, accounts payable, accounts receivable, purchasing, and all other staff support functions to be intimately involved in the quality improvement process.

3M's investigation reemphasized the importance and interrelationship of each function within the organization. It became apparent that external customers provided a quality product or service through the efforts of a series of internal "customers," each of whom receives the work or "product" of another internal person and passes it on to another person. It is the responsibility of each internal person to determine the expectations of their "customer" and to find out from that customer specific areas where they are not meeting that customer's expectations. In this way, each person and function within 3M, from research and development to production, right through marketing, sales, and distribution, influences the quality of 3M's products and services — no matter how far removed they are from the final product delivered to the user.

3. *Quality is attained through prevention-oriented improvement projects.* The third key concept in 3M's strategy is prevention. 3M adopted a new quality system that involves identifying the cause of errors, and then implementing specific projects to change the process, procedure, or materials to prevent errors from recurring. The system of prevention replaces the system of inspection, which is inspecting and sorting through mistakes *after* they have occurred.

A. V. Feigenbaum, a noted quality authority, estimated that as much as 15 to 40 percent of production capacity may exist solely to rework, retest, or reinspect rejected units. The same holds true for work done in nonmanufacturing areas such as marketing, finance, and administration.

4. *The objective is consistent conformance to expectations 100 percent of the time rather than management's acceptance of anything less.* This concept is perhaps the most difficult to understand and accept. Traditionally, 3M has set performance standards with the attitude that errors are inevitable. In production operations this attitude has fostered the AQL (acceptable quality level). An AQL standard, in effect, establishes a projected failure rate before an operation is even begun. It is hardly surprising, then, that these predictions usually occur. An AQL mentality hides most of the real costs associated with error. However, properly identifying and measuring these costs and implementing a quality improvement process based on prevention and a 100 percent conformance standard will eliminate problems and errors.

Causes of nonconformance are identified and corrected forever, so that the product or service more consistently meets customer requirements, thus benefiting both the customer and the balance sheet.

5. *Measurements of quality are through indicators of customer satisfaction, rather than indicators of self-gratification.* Companies often get caught up in measurements of certain activities that make the company look good on paper yet reveal little meaningful information on how well it is competing on a quality basis in its markets. These are indicators of self-gratification — measurements that management, owners, and stockholders like to see and that seem to say that their investments are being used productively.

While such indices have their use, 3M has adopted a set of quality measurements that directly relate to its effectiveness in satisfying customers' expectations. These measurements include returns, lost business, sales adjustments, on-time deliveries, missed deadlines (external and internal), exception reports, and overtime worked. By focusing on these kinds of measurements, 3M obtains a more accurate picture of its customers' level of satisfaction with products and services and how well 3M is satisfying their expectations. Many companies are using cost of quality as a measure of quality improvement. This can easily lead to making quality another cost-reduction program.

Quality Implementation Strategy

3M began implementing the total quality improvement process by developing a 3M quality policy statement to communicate its commitment and direction of quality emphasis to employees and external publics. The statement is a combination of corporate policy and corporate objectives: "3M will develop, produce, and deliver, on time, products and services that conform to customer expectations."

3M's quality policy also spells out specifically what is meant by conformance to expectations: "These products and services must be useful, safe, reliable, environmentally acceptable, and represented truthfully in advertising, packaging, and sales promotions."

An implementation statement accompanies the quality policy, to affirm that 3M will manage its business to ensure that "conformance to expectations" is the goal of the entire company. This statement also identifies specific objectives:

- 3M will measure the cost of quality in all departments, divisions, groups, business sectors, and international subsidiaries.
- 3M will ensure conformance to personal, product, service, and regulatory requirements on a worldwide basis.
- 3M will communicate its commitment to quality to our customers (through policy and performance).

Translating the policy and objectives into an operational activity is an enormous undertaking, complicated by 3M's size and diversity. It became obvious early on that the best way to implement the improvement process was to provide guidelines and methods that can be adapted and modified to suit the culture, problems, and personality of each operating area.

Formal training for all supervisory and management personnel became 3M's first step in internalizing the quality process. Initial training involved a two and one-half-day workshop that covered the five essentials of quality identified earlier.

The improvement process has four phases to be accomplished. In the first phase, management works through a planning stage to gain an understanding and awareness of quality as it applies to their individual environment.

For the second phase, management forms a quality improvement team made up of representatives from each major function and key staff people who provide critical resources. The QST has the responsibility for identifying major improvement opportunities and developing a specific action plan to achieve them.

The third phase involves the creation of on-site or sub-QST teams in each area of operation, either to work on all or portions of a problem or opportunity for improvement directed by the corporate QST, or to take action on secondary problems more closely related to their specific area.

The fourth phase involves identifying errors, measuring the cost of quality and setting goals and objectives to correct errors. It is at this phase that actual quality improvement begins. Identifying errors and the costs associated with making errors provides an important index for quantifying conformance, prioritizing opportunities for improvement that will provide the greatest return, and measuring improvement that occurs.

Quality-related costs fall into three broad categories:

1. Cost of appraisal — those costs associated with testing and inspection.
2. Cost of failure — those costs associated with the internal or external failure of a product or service. Failure costs go well beyond the obvious ones, such as waste in production, to include all the time and money involved in reworking or correcting errors in all functions. An example is reprinting a brochure or changing a proposal to correct an error, where not only material costs but lost time and even lost business must be measured.
3. Cost of prevention — those costs necessary to correct a process or procedure to ensure that work is done right the first time and consistent conformance to customer expectations is achieved.

3M's goal is to reduce appraisal and failure costs continually, recognizing that in doing so there will be some increase in prevention costs.

Management Training

Whenever possible, training is conducted for the management group of each business unit. This has helped to promote the discussion of specific problems and to emphasize the interrelationship of each function in achieving quality improvement. Phase I training exposes management to a new awareness of quality and promotes a changed attitude in evaluating the business and its operations.

Concurrent with quality workshop training, the staff quality department supports the improvement process on a three-prong basis:

1. Quality managers are assigned to work with each business unit to help implement quality concepts and the improvement process.
2. A systems group sets up criteria to measure current cost of quality within each unit and for the company as a whole.
3. A quality circle support staff provides the training and tools necessary to allow nonmanagement personnel to participate in solving problems they can control, or to suggest solutions to management where higher approval is required.

Roadblocks to Quality

It would be ideal if, after completing the quality workshop training, each unit was able to implement the new quality philosophy immediately and completely to solve problems and take advantage of opportunities for improvement. Although there is some demonstration of success in a variety of areas, there is also a wide range of roadblocks, some that are expected and others that come as a surprise.

Some of the more frequent obstacles and the methods used to remove them are listed as follows:

Escalating cost of quality. Initial programs that resulted in cost reductions were offset by overall increases in the cost of corporate-wide quality. This was due to the fact that initial cost of quality estimates were based only on the most obvious and easy-to-measure factors. As the quality process progressed, the cost of nonconformance in areas that were previously unmeasureable were able to be isolated and identified.

Quality outside the factory. As most of the successes by the Japanese have been achieved and documented within factory or production environments, it is not surprising that 3M also experienced many of its initial improvements in this area. Historically, a factory functions within a wide range of standards, measurement methods, and well-defined processes, more so than any other business operation. Initiating programs for improvement in the factory was easier as many of the opportunities were more obvious and in many cases the indices for measurement were already in place.

Implementing the process in less rigid areas, such as marketing, laboratory, administration, and staff groups, was a more difficult task. Many times the "product" produced in these environments is so interrelated with other functions or so poorly defined that it is difficult to identify the problem and even more difficult to break it into manageable segments for improvement. Applying traditional measurement indices further complicates the process, as in many instances specific dollar measurements have never been applied or the costs are hidden in a myriad of other categories.

It soon became obvious that to extend quality improvement beyond the factory, additional techniques and methods were needed. We developed a Phase II training package that included the philosophy and tools of such quality experts as Deming, Juran, Feigenbaum, Ishikawa, and others.

Phase II tools include a wide range of statistical and analytical techniques to promote brainstorming, data gathering, data analysis, presentation of information, control, and prioritization.

Some of these tools include:

- Pareto diagrams
- Cause-and-effect diagrams (often called Ishikawa or fishbone diagrams)
- Check sheets of various kinds
- Histograms
- Functional analysis
- Flow charts
- Process dissection
- Nominal group technique brainstorming (NGT)
- Scatter diagrams
- Control charts
- Gantt charts
- Process capability studies
- Probability plotting

Rather than train every area on all techniques, 3M's strategy is to tailor Phase II training to suit the requirements of each individual area. Quality specialists work closely with business units to determine the most appropriate tools to apply to the specific problems being addressed.

These methods improve 3M's ability to isolate hard costs associated with non-production activities such as order entry, marketing, and so on. Where hard costs are still not a viable measurement, other criteria such as time and people, which ultimately translate to dollars, are used.

Teams

Analyzing "products and customers" emphasized the importance of team efforts. It became obvious that quality objectives could not be achieved without personal commitments to quality and a group commitment to work together for improvement.

Teamwork, however, is not a natural working method. It must be learned. 3M, like most American companies, had systems in place to emphasize and reward individual efforts and achievements more than group accomplishments. Undertaking quality improvement projects on a team basis required new insights into group behavior, from top management through quality circles of hourly workers. The 3M human resources department offered a multitude of courses and techniques on group processes, group dynamics, and group motivation to better understand the functions, needs, and processes of group activity. Working with human resources personnel to tie group training and new management techniques, such as performance management, to tangible programs that are quality related, has accelerated the integration of both processes within the company.

Plateaus

It is not uncommon to see a business unit make tremendous headway on a number of quality projects, then suddenly flounder in an attempt to establish a next goal. Solutions to this dilemma range from rotating people on the QST and action teams, to surveying employees to identify reasons for lack of interest or to generate new ideas for improvement to trying any of the new techniques available, to simple recommitting to quality as a group.

As a corporation, 3M constantly interfaces with outside companies and experts to identify other tools and ideas to expand our scope and ability to assist improvement.

Time

Perhaps the most common barrier encountered in quality improvement is time — the time needed to involve already busy people and schedules to identify areas to improve and the time necessary to implement corrective action. There is no question that allocating time for quality improvement requires management's belief and commitment that improvement will reduce costs and increase productivity and ultimately, provide more time for productive uses. Effort spent resolving crises can be reduced, as the causes of the fires are identified and eliminated forever. Once an area achieves its first success, it is much easier to gain time commitments for further projects. For this reason, it is important to keep initial goals realistic and attainable.

Another way in which 3M has overcome the time issue is to integrate quality with other corporate policies and procedures. Such things as making quality a part of the annual performance appraisal makes each employee more cognizant of his or her responsibility to improve individual performance. Annual quality plans are drafted to ensure ongoing improvement, and the corporation asks each division to include quality as part of their business and strategic plans.

Tied to existing practices, quality improvement becomes a part of our daily business operations and goals, not a separate process to be allocated special time.

Attitude

It would be naive to expect that any group of more than 80,000 individuals will accept and internalize a new philosophy at exactly the same pace or in the same manner. And of course, that has not happened at 3M. But the success of those who have been active in the improvement process has had a snowball effect. Continued promotion and awareness internally of those successes, ongoing training in improvement techniques, and the support and direction of top management have all had a dramatic impact on creating the necessary attitude change and involvement.

Successes

In the few years since 3M began the total quality improvement process, we have achieved improvements ranging from dollar savings to minor procedural changes that improve morale and the work environment. Regardless of the scope of individual successes, each is recognized as an important contribution to quality improvement.

Today, over 60 percent of 3M's management and supervisory staff worldwide has been trained in quality improvement concepts, and more than two-thirds of our division and staff groups have active quality improvement processes in place. Plans are moving to educate the remaining management personnel and to work more closely with areas not yet active.

3M currently has 1,013 active quality circles solving work-related problems in all areas of the company. These circles, made up of volunteer employees at all job levels, have not only yielded dollar savings, but have gone a long way in promoting quality awareness throughout the corporation.

Quality – A Positive Business Strategy

Quality is an enormous business opportunity to impact growth through keeping a competitive edge in the marketplace. In addition to product performance, the competitive edge will also include service and all interactions with the customers before and after the sale.

Cost of quality impact on profits and price can also help remain competitive and finance growth.

The quality process must be continuous. This requires a constant flow of training, new techniques, and teams to keep the competitive edge strong. All of the experts in quality can contribute to the quality improvement process depending on the needs of each business. Total quality leadership is hard work and there are no substitutes and no shortcuts.

The quality improvement process must remain strong well into the future. Those who persist will be leaders while others falter in the highly competitive global marketplace.